Road Biking™ Massachusetts

Help Us Keep This Guide Up to Date

Every effort has been made by the author and editors to make this guide as accurate and useful as possible. However, many things can change after a guide is published—trails are rerouted, regulations change, techniques evolve, facilities come under new management, etc.

We would love to hear from you concerning your experiences with this guide and how you feel it could be improved and kept up to date. While we may not be able to respond to all comments and suggestions, we'll take them to heart, and we'll also make certain to share them with the authors. Please send your comments and suggestions to the following address:

The Globe Pequot Press
Reader Response/Editorial Department
P.O. Box 480
Guilford, CT 06437

Or you may e-mail us at:

editorial@GlobePequot.com

Thanks for your input, and happy trails!

A **FALCON** GUIDE®

Road Biking™ Series

Road Biking™
Massachusetts

A Guide to the Greatest Bike Rides in Massachusetts

Tom Catalini

FALCON GUIDE®

GUILFORD, CONNECTICUT
HELENA, MONTANA

AN IMPRINT OF THE GLOBE PEQUOT PRESS

To Stephanie, for all her love, support, and friendship.

For Alec, Mia, and Annalise, for all the love, joy, and energy they bring to life.

AFALCONGUIDE®□

Copyright © 2007 Morris Book Publishing, LLC

Falcon and FalconGuide are registered trademarks and
Road Biking is a trademark of Morris Book Publishing, LLC.

Photos by Tom Catalini except where noted
Spine photo © Chuck Haney
Maps by Trailhead Graphics © Morris Book Publishing, LLC

Library of Congress Cataloging-in-Publication Data
Catalini, Tom.
  Road biking Massachusetts/Tom Catalini.—1st ed.
      p. cm.—(Road biking series)
  ISBN-13: 978-0-7627-3909-7
  ISBN-10: 0-7627-3909-6
 1. Cycling—Massachusetts—Guidebooks. 2.
Massachusetts—Guidebooks. I. Title. II. Series.
  GV1045.5.M4C38 2006
  796.6'409744—dc22
                                        2006011730

Manufactured in the United States of America
First Edition/Fourth Printing

Contents

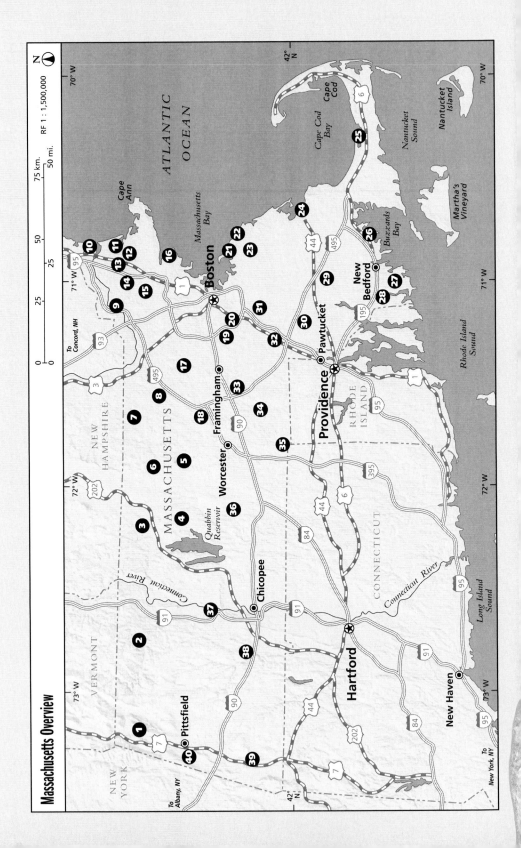

Massachusetts Overview

RF 1 : 1,500,000

Preface

Massachusetts abounds with terrain, culture, and history conducive to cycling enjoyment! From the towering peaks of the rugged Berkshire Mountains to the tip of the generous Cape Cod coastline, there is plenty of fun to be had for the enthusiastic cyclist. The state's rich history and unique place in America's birth provide a wealth of interesting and important sites to see. With a tremendous number of active cyclists, Massachusetts also enjoys a wealth of active and well-organized clubs and many advocates who work hard to develop local legislation for safer riding conditions and an impressive array of bike trails.

Choosing rides to include in this book was fun, but not easy. The forty rides were carefully selected to give the best sampling of the diverse offerings Massachusetts has for the cyclist. Special attention was given to the time-tested roads and routes of the many active clubs in the state, access to provisions along the routes, and most of all, safety. Generally speaking, the western half of the state is more rugged and rural and the eastern half flatter and more developed.

My deep gratitude goes to the many great clubs that provide companionship, expertise, and inspiration, notably the Northeast Bicycle Club, the Charles River Wheelmen, the North Shore Cyclists, and the Gringo Riders. Most of the shorter rides in this book were originally mapped out in whole or in part by Howard Stone, to whom I extend my sincere thanks. Many longer routes were inspired by popular club rides. Routes that closely follow annual or recurring club rides have been noted so that you could consider joining a group along one of the routes, which is always more fun than going it alone.

Special thanks to Tim Stansel, who accompanied me on many scouting missions, and to Kevin Aldrich, John Trainor, Bob Gaylord, Pete Muir, Robb Hewitt, and Jeff Cordisco, who were also very patient companions and willing explorers. Their enthusiasm and friendship made the effort fun.

It seems appropriate to note here the origins of my passion for cycling, which ultimately led me to this point. I joined the ranks of the Pan Mass Challenge bike-a-thon to benefit cancer research after having lost my dad to cancer. The ride is an inspirational and gratifying event. It's also a serious cycling challenge. I would not have made it through that first 200-mile journey, however, if not for the camaraderie and support of my brothers Mike and Mark, and for the patience and inspiration of Mike Fairhurst, who showed us all the ropes. My brothers and I continue to do the PMC ride each year, now unfortunately also in memory of our mom, also lost to cancer.

I'd like to also thank Bill Schneider and all the folks at Globe Pequot Press for all their hard work in editing this book and for developing stunning graphics for each route, as well as for taking a chance on a first-time author. Jim Homerosky, author of two other Road Biking guides, also provided a wealth of sage advice which helped me out tremendously. Thanks, Jim.

Most of all, thanks to my wife, Stephanie, who helped and supported me along the way, with this and with everything. And also to my children, Alec, Mia, and Annalise, who were always patient and understanding when I had to put the extra time into this work. I hope to ride these routes with you someday!

Introduction

Biking in Massachusetts

Massachusetts is magnificent for cycling. You don't have to look very far to find an active cycling group for guidance and companionship, interesting sites to visit, and appealing terrain to navigate. Challenges abound among the mountains of western Massachusetts, the hills of central Massachusetts, and, of course, the abundant seacoast of eastern Massachusetts.

Riding in the Berkshires is challenging, but rewarding. Perhaps the most scenic and rural rides in the book lie in this western outpost of the state. Here you will find the state's highest point atop Mount Greylock and unique villages that were home to some of the state's more famous artistic citizens, such as Normal Rockwell and Herman Melville. When cycling in this part of the state, it's easy to see how one could be profoundly inspired.

East of the mighty Connecticut River and west of the Interstate 495 beltway is central Massachusetts. The less mountainous but still extremely hilly area surrounding the man-made Quabbin Reservoir is just as scenic and rural as western Massachusetts, without the long, dramatic climbs the of the mountains, though you will eventually find that Mount Wachusett beckons to be climbed. Mount Wachusett, just east of the Quabbin, offers a climb as tough as any in the Berkshires and shines as the centerpiece of the annual Fitchburg Lonsjo Classic bike race each July. On the eastern side of central Massachusetts, you'll find wonderful rolling hills and challenging climbs up Nashoba Valley and into New Hampshire in the north and similarly challenging and historic landscape in the Pioneer Valley of the south.

Eastern Massachusetts offers a wealth of fun, scenic, and flatter rides, often convenient to major highway access. As such, this is where the majority of the rides in the book are laid out. Interestingly, it's not hard to find rural and scenic roads just off the beaten path in eastern Massachusetts, and many challenging hills still ripple through to the inside of the I–495 beltway. As the birthplace of the American Revolution, the area that stretches from the site of the "shot heard around the world" in Concord to the site of the Boston Tea Party on the Boston waterfront is rich in history and sites to visit. Also unique to the eastern side of the state is the scenic coastline. Its jagged shape and unique 80-mile-long Cape Cod peninsula offer many wonderful opportunities to ride alongside the Atlantic Ocean.

Whatever type of cycling adventure or challenge you seek can be found in Massachusetts. It is my hope that this guide exposes you to new cycling opportunities across the state and inspires you to go out and ride. See you on the road.

Road and Traffic Conditions

Massachusetts is well developed with an intricate web of highways and busier roads. This will make it convenient for you to easily reach different parts of the state by car, but it can also present occasional hazards to cyclists. Most of the rides in this book are along secondary roads, but sometimes crossing a major throughway or riding a short segment along a busier road is unavoidable.

Riding conditions vary depending on the time of year and time of day. Massachusetts experiences the full effect of all four seasons in New England. Snowstorms can appear quickly in the winter time, and conditions can change dramatically while out on the road. You'll need to be on the lookout for black ice. Extremely dangerous to cyclists, black ice can appear anytime it is cold after a rain storm or snow melt, particularly in the early morning or evening hours. If you ride in the spring, watch out for frost heaves and potholes created by winter conditions and plowing. Summer perhaps offers some of the best conditions for cycling in Massachusetts, but it can get very hot in July and August. Also, thunderstorms can and do appear suddenly. Fall offers wonderful foliage to view, which of course can create another hazard—obstacles hidden under fallen and sometimes slippery leaves.

Seasonal areas will also attract more people and heavier traffic. It may be best to avoid rides near beaches in hot weather or in the Berkshires during peak foliage-viewing times. Generally speaking, it is also best to avoid riding during early morning or late afternoon commute times along most of the routes in the eastern half of the state. Quaint areas such as historic Concord and Lexington take on dramatically different personalities during these times. It's best to ride these areas on the weekends.

Safety and Comfort on the Road

Massachusetts laws governing cycling are similar to most other states. Cyclists are required to ride on the right side of the road, with the flow of traffic. Cyclists may ride on road shoulders but are not permitted to ride on interstate highways and other controlled-access highways. Hand signals are required (using either hand is ok) and riders must ride single file unless passing. Riders younger than age sixteen must wear a helmet, though it is strongly recommended that you always wear your helmet when riding your bike.

Every bicycle ridden between sunset and sunrise must have proper lighting. Your headlight must be white and visible from a distance of at least 500 feet. Your taillight must be red and visible from a distance of at least 600 feet. Reflectors must be visible in the low beams of a car's headlights, and if your pedals don't have reflectors, you must wear reflective bracelets on both ankles. Reflectors must be visible from both your front and back and from your sides. Bicycles ridden on roadways must have brakes that will bring you to a stop from a speed of 15 miles an hour within 30 feet of braking on dry, level, clean pavement.

Most importantly, it is best to adopt a defensive riding style. Stop at all stop signs and red lights, and keep an eye out for motorists making illegal or sudden turns into your path. Keep an eye out for doors that can pop open suddenly from parked cars, or cars that may pull away from the curb suddenly. Don't use headphones or other devices that will limit your ability to hear vehicles approaching from behind or other hazards that may be outside of your field of vision.

Remember to have your bike inspected and tuned up at least twice a year by a professional mechanic. Also, make sure you are prepared for the most common problems that can occur out on the road, such as a flat tire (always pack two tubes!) or broken spoke. You would also be well advised to carry a chain tool for the rarer, but debilitating chain break. Also be sure to always carry identification, cash, a credit card, and a cell phone if you have one. These will be handy if you need to hire a cab, rent a car, or take other action in the event of a major problem.

Cycling clothes can help to increase comfort while in the saddle. Not only do bike jerseys provide increased visibility, but their fabric helps wick perspiration and keep you dry. They usually are equipped with convenient rear pockets to carry supplies and a longer cut in back to provide adequate cover in the stretched-out position. Padded shorts may look funny and invite stares, but they definitely reduce saddle soreness and protect your inner thighs from chaffing. Biking shorts are one item that you never want to compromise on.

Finally, always carry at least one water bottle with you. A good rule is to drink one bottle of water for every hour of cycling. Alternating between water and sports drinks is also often recommended to be sure that you take in enough electrolytes during your ride. It's also a good idea to carry energy bars, Fig Newtons, or a bagel or banana with you. Review the Miles and Directions section of a ride before you head out to know beforehand if stores are available and where they are located.

How to Use This Book

The forty routes in *Road Biking Massachusetts* are divided into four categories according to degree of difficulty. These classifications are subjective, taking into account the combination of distance, road grade, and bike-handling skills necessary to negotiate the full tour. Each route's name indicates its relative degree of difficulty.

Rambles are the easiest and shortest rides in the book, accessible to almost all riders, and they should be completed easily in one day. They are usually less than 35 miles long and are generally on flat to slightly rolling terrain.

Cruises are intermediate in difficulty and distance. They are generally 25 to 50 miles long and may include some moderate climbs. Cruises generally will be completed easily by an experienced rider in one day, but inexperienced or out-of-shape riders may want to take two days with an overnight stop.

Challenges are difficult, and they are designed especially for experienced riders in good condition. They're usually 40 to 60 miles long and may include some steep climbs. They should be a challenge even for fairly fit riders attempting to complete them in one day. Less-experienced or less-fit riders should expect to take two days.

Classics are long and hard. They are more than 60 miles and may be more than 100 miles long. They can include steep climbs and high-speed descents. Even fit and experienced riders will want to take two days to complete these rides, which are not recommended for less-fit and less-experienced riders unless they are done in shorter stages.

Remember that terrain is as much a factor as distance in determining a ride's category. The 53-mile South Shore Coastal Cruise is actually a lot easier than the shorter 36-mile Hilltown Challenge. Examining the elevation profile of a ride together with the distance will enable you to select rides most appropriate for your ability level.

Don't let the distance of a longer tour dissuade you from trying a ride in an attractive area. Out-and-back rides along portions of a route provide options that may be well suited to your schedule and other commitments. Likewise, don't automatically dismiss a shorter ride in an interesting area.

Directions in the route narrative for each ride include the cumulative mileage to each turn and to significant landmarks along the way. It's possible that your mileage may differ slightly. Over enough miles, differences in odometer calibration, tire pressure, and the line you follow can have a significant effect on the measurement of distance. Use the cumulative mileage in connection with your route descriptions and maps to calculate route distances.

The selection of these routes is the result of extensive reading and research, suggestions from bike shops, cycling clubs, friends, and local experts, and a lot of bicycling. Some of the routes are well-known cycling venues; others are less frequently ridden. Taken as a whole, the routes in this book are intended to offer a cross section of the best riding location in the state, indicative of the wide variety of roads and terrain Massachusetts has to offer.

Members of the Gringo Riders at the Convenient Mann in Dunstable on the Lunenburg Cruise

To the greatest extent possible, each route has been designed with specific criteria in mind, although not all criteria could be addressed in every instance. Starting points are normally easy to find, with convenient parking and reasonable access to provisions. Roads should be moderately traveled, be in good repair, and have adequate shoulders where traffic volume requires. I've also made an effort to guide the reader to interesting places along the way.

To fashion the most useful routes, some worthwhile features were bypassed for practical considerations. As a result, you might find it appropriate to use these routes as starting points or suggestions in designing your own routes. Rides can begin at any point along the course described in the route directions. You can always leave the route to explore interesting side roads and create your own routes.

Construction, development, improvements, and other changes are commonplace on Massachusetts roadways. As a result, the route descriptions and maps in this book may be only records of conditions as they once were; they may not always describe conditions as you find them. Comments, updates, and corrections from interested and critical readers are always welcome and appreciated, and can be sent to the author in care of the publisher.

Map Legend

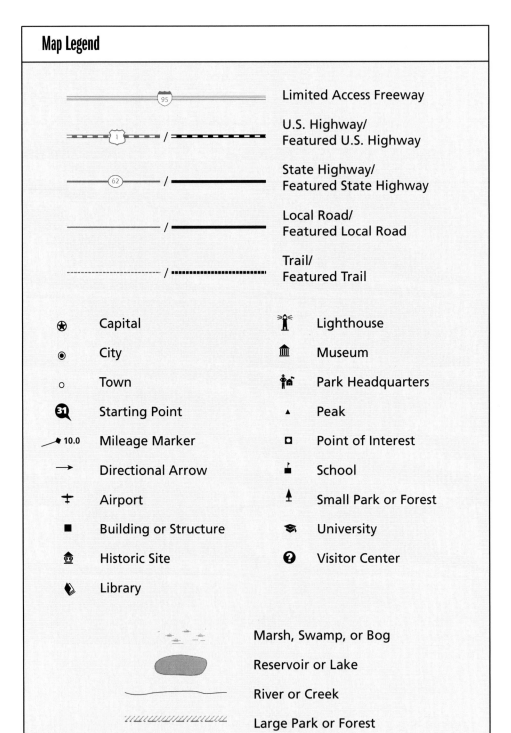

Limited Access Freeway

U.S. Highway/
Featured U.S. Highway

State Highway/
Featured State Highway

Local Road/
Featured Local Road

Trail/
Featured Trail

⊛ Capital

◉ City

○ Town

㉛ Starting Point

10.0 Mileage Marker

→ Directional Arrow

✛ Airport

■ Building or Structure

🏛 Historic Site

📖 Library

🗼 Lighthouse

🏛 Museum

🧍 Park Headquarters

▲ Peak

▫ Point of Interest

▪ School

🌲 Small Park or Forest

🎓 University

❓ Visitor Center

Marsh, Swamp, or Bog

Reservoir or Lake

River or Creek

Large Park or Forest

State Boundary

1 Mount Greylock Challenge

Climb it because it is there. When you summit Mount Greylock, you will be reaching the highest point in all of Massachusetts, where you can enjoy spectacular 360-degree views of the Berkshires. Unclip and climb the Veterans War Memorial at the summit to fully soak it all in. This challenging ride will bring you from Pittsfield to the summit in the first third of the ride. After completing the brake-burning descent (which requires great care and patience), you'll head over to Williamstown, a quaint town that is home to Williams College. The second half of the route takes you south through the valley, giving you a rest and a chance to appreciate the mountain range from a different perspective while climbing back toward Pittsfield at a more moderate pace. Plan to do the ride during the spring or summer as the Mount Greylock Scenic Byway is accessible only from mid-May through mid-October.

Start: Allendale Shopping Center, Pittsfield.
Length: 52.1 miles.
Ride time: 4 to 5 hours.
Terrain: Very hilly with a mountain summit climb.
Traffic and hazards: SR 8 sections can be busy, but there is a wide shoulder. State Route 2 is busy, and traffic can be heavy in downtown Williamstown. The Greylock climb and decent can be busy on weekends as Greylock is a popular tourist spot. The ideal time for this ride is early in the morning or on a weekday.

Getting there: From the Massachusetts Turnpike, follow U.S. Route 20 to Pittsfield, where it will merge with U.S. Route 7. In the center of Pittsfield, US 7 and US 20 split; stay on US 7 through the center of town. Turn right (east) onto State Route 9 (Tyler Street), which begins at the far end of town. Travel approximately 3 miles and when SR 9 merges with State Route 8 North, stay in the left lane for SR 8 North. (McDonald's is on the left.) Turn into the Allendale Shopping Center parking lot.

The Berkshires is a wonderful area for a variety of outdoor activities, particularly cycling. This ride will take you through some spectacular roads and offer up some challenging climbs. Though not the toughest ascent in Massachusetts, climbing the south face of Mount Greylock will bring you to the highest point in the state—3,491 feet above sea level. In addition to its unique stature in height, Mount Greylock is also the flagship of the Massachusetts state park system. Mount Greylock became the first state park of Massachusetts in 1898 after 800 acres were given to the commonwealth by the Greylock Park Association. Today the reservation has expanded to 12,500 acres and includes more than 70 miles of hiking trails.

Departing from Pittsfield, you'll quickly escape to quiet country roads and have just enough time to warm up before starting the summit climb. Don't be discouraged by the super-steep grades at the very start of the climb. Approaching the Mount Greylock Visitors Center is the toughest part of the ascent. Do take time to stop in,

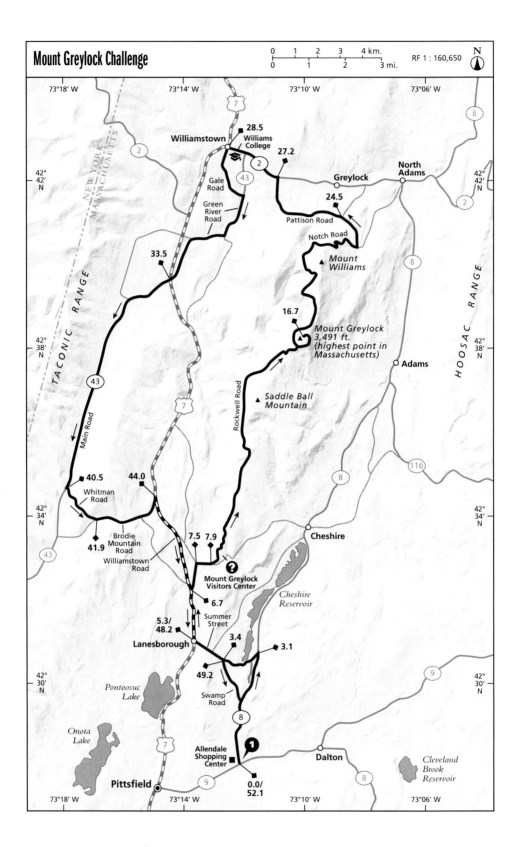

Mount Greylock Challenge

RF 1 : 160,650

not only to catch your breath but also to see the fantastic three-dimensional map of the mountain range that fills up the lobby area. The center also provides restrooms and water fountains.

You'll be surprised to find two downhill sections along the rest of this climb as you traverse the mountain range on your way to Greylock, going up and over the shoulder of Saddle Ball Mountain. These short downhills provide some great relief along the way to the top. Once you reach the summit, it's well worth making the extra effort to unclip and walk up the spiral staircase to the top of the 92-foot-high Veterans War Memorial, dedicated to the state in 1933, for fantastic panoramic views of the Berkshires. Here you can look down on the valley you'll be traversing on the second half of the route.

Another jewel of the summit is the Bascom Lodge, built in 1937 by the Civilian Conservation Corps, an organization created by President Roosevelt during the Great Depression. The rustic lodge has a snack bar, seating, and restrooms for the public. The lodge can also accommodate up to thirty-two overnight guests and offers family-style dinner service.

Descending Greylock's north face is a real brake burner. The roads are in rough shape, with many potholes and frost heaves. Go slowly and use caution. You may even need to stop once or twice to rest your arms from holding your brakes. The descent is steady for nearly 7 miles and very steep in sections.

Once you're at the bottom, you'll enjoy some great flat sections on the way to North Adams. About halfway through the ride, you'll be in downtown Williamstown right by Williams College. There are many restaurants and convenience stores for food and drinks. Papa Charlie's deli is a good stop with a wide variety of sandwiches, many of them named after celebrities, such as Dick Cavett, Bo Derek, and Richard Chamberlain.

From downtown Williamstown, you'll traverse the valley along State Route 43, enjoying great rolling hills and breathtaking views of the mountain range, which is comprised of Mount Williams, Mount Fitch, Mount Prospect, and Ragged Mountain in addition to Greylock. Enjoy the respite from the major climbs while you can because there's one more serious climbing section before you reach the end of the ride.

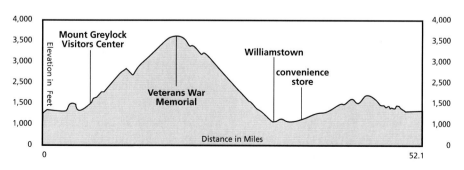

Miles and Directions

0.0 Turn left out of Allendale Shopping Center onto SR 8 North (busy road).

3.1 Turn left onto Old State Road (white church on corner).

3.4 Turn right onto Summer Street.

5.3 Turn right onto US 7 North.

6.7 Turn right onto North Main Street and follow signs for Mount Greylock.

7.5 Turn right onto Quarry Road (not marked but there are MOUNT GREYLOCK STATE RESERVATION signs).

7.9 Turn left onto Rockwell Road. Very steep ascent to the visitors center. Follow signs to the summit.

16.7 Summit! Veterans War Memorial.

17.5 Turn right onto Notch Road as you descend from the summit (very steep, use caution).

24.5 Proceed straight onto Pattison Road (Notch Road turns right here); the reservoir will be on your left.

27.2 Turn left onto SR 2 West (busy road).

28.5 Turn left onto Spring Street (downtown Williamstown—shops, restaurants).

28.9 Turn right onto SR 43.

33.5 Continue straight over US 7 (The Store at Five Corners convenience store).

40.5 Turn left onto Whitman Road.

41.9 Turn left onto Brodie Mountain Road.

44.0 Turn right onto US 7 South.

48.2 Turn left onto Summer Street.

49.2 Turn right onto Partridge Road.

49.3 Turn left onto Swamp Road.

50.2 Turn right at stop sign onto Old State Road (not marked).

50.5 Turn right onto SR 8 South.

52.1 Arrive back at Allendale Shopping Center.

Ride Information

Local Information

The Berkshire Visitors Bureau, 3 Hoosac Street, Adams; (800) 237-5747 or (413) 743-4500; www.berkshires.org.

Mount Greylock State Reservation, Rockwell Road, Lanesborough; (413) 499-4262.

Pittsfield Visitors Center, 121 South Street, Pittsfield; (413) 395-0105.

Local Events/Attractions

Strawberry Festival, Williamstown in June.

Restaurants

Papa Charlie's Deli & Juice Bar, 28 Spring Street, Williamstown; (413) 458-5969.

Accommodations

Bascom Lodge, Summit of Mount Greylock, Adams; (413) 743-1591.

Berkshire Inn Motel, 150 Housatonic Street, Pittsfield; (800) 443-0633 or (413) 443-3000.

Ramada Limited Inn & Suites, 1350 West Housatonic Street, Pittsfield; (877) 477-5817.

2 Shelburne Falls Challenge

The Shelburne Falls Challenge is not for the timid. With more than 4,300 feet of climbing in just 50 miles, this tour of unspoiled small towns will take some effort. Far from any metropolitan area, the landscape is very rural, with virtually no traffic except for a couple of crossings at State Route 2 and Interstate 91, as well as a brief stretch on SR 2 near the end of the ride. You'll traverse a harmonious mix of woods and farmland, with hills rising in the distance across the fields.

Start: Municipal parking lot on Water Street in Shelburne Falls across from Bottle of Bread.
Length: 50.3 miles.
Ride time: 3 to 4 hours.
Terrain: Very hilly with three big climbs.

Traffic and hazards: Quiet country roads except for some busy crossings and a heavily trafficked section through Greenfield center and briefly along SR 2 at the end of the ride.

Getting there: From SR 2 West, turn left onto State Route 2A West for 0.6 mile. Turn right onto Water Street immediately before the bridge, and the parking lot is just ahead on the right. From SR 2 East, turn right onto SR 2A East for 0.7 mile. Turn left and cross the bridge and turn left onto Water Street. Parking lot is just ahead on the right.

The ride starts from Shelburne Falls, an attractive town with galleries and craft shops gracing the handsome brick buildings in the downtown area. The town spans both sides of the Deerfield River, although most of the activity is on the east bank. Crossing the river is the lovely Bridge of Flowers, a pedestrian bridge lined with plants and flowers on both sides. Built as a trolley bridge in 1908, it carried trolleys until 1928. A small trolley museum stands at the east end of the bridge, across the street from the starting point.

Another attraction in Shelburne Falls is the Glacial Potholes, a cluster of circular holes carved into the rocks along the riverbed by the swirling of water throughout millions of years. The larger potholes are perfect swimming holes in hot weather and a great spot to cool off after the ride.

When you leave Shelburne Falls, you'll head north to Leyden and the first two big climbs of the ride before spinning down into Greenfield. If it's mid-July, don't be surprised if you see hot-air balloons floating through the air. The Green River Festival, begun as a balloon festival and transformed into a full-fledged music festival, has been a popular western Massachusetts event since its inception in 1986.

Picturesque farm along the Shelburne Falls Challenge route

From Greenfield you'll follow the Deerfield River, climbing gradually through hillside farms and then descending into Conway, a small village with a handsome domed library. You'll pass the Conway Covered Bridge, built in 1869, a short distance west of town. It is closed to traffic.

From Conway, it's all uphill to Ashfield—gradually at first as you follow the South River upstream and then steeply for the last half mile into town. Ashfield is a pristine New England village with two white churches, a fine stone library, and a graceful town hall with a bell tower. A historic landmark in town is the Zachariah Field Tavern (now a house), a long red building dating from 1792. Just past Ashfield you'll ride along Ashfield Lake, where there's a small beach and a snack bar.

From Ashfield it's all downhill to Buckland, a nearly undiscovered village tucked away on a side road off State Route 112. Here you'll ride past some handsome old houses, a traditional white church, a small brick library, and a historical museum. From Buckland it's several flat miles back to Shelburne Falls through the valley of the Deerfield River; you'll follow the river closely at the end.

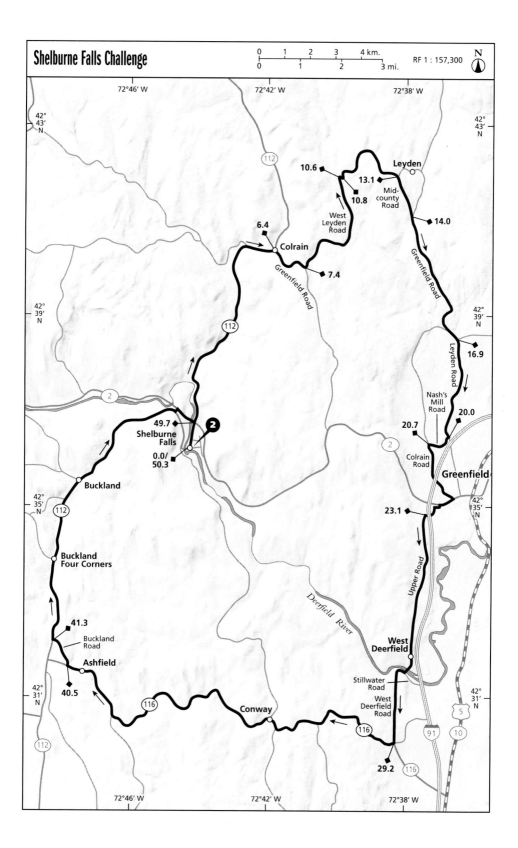

Shelburne Falls Challenge

RF 1 : 157,300

Miles and Directions

0.0 Depart municipal parking lot.

0.2 Turn left onto Main Street.

0.5 Keep straight onto SR 112 (Main Street).

6.4 Bear right onto Greenfield Road.

7.4 Turn left onto West Leyden Road.

10.6 Turn right to stay on West Leyden Road.

10.8 Turn left to stay on West Leyden Road.

13.1 Keep straight onto Mid-county Road.

14.0 Keep straight onto Greenfield Road.

16.9 Road name changes to Leyden Road.

20.0 Turn right onto Nash's Mill Road.

20.7 Turn left onto Colrain Road.

22.1 Turn left onto SR 2 (Mohawk Trail).

22.2 At roundabout, take the first exit onto SR 2A (Mohawk Trail).

22.6 Turn right onto Newton Street.

22.7 Turn left onto Fairview Street West.

23.1 Turn left onto Munson Street.

23.8 Road name changes to Upper Road.

27.1 Turn right onto Stillwater Road.

27.7 Road name changes to West Deerfield Road (Stillwater Road).

29.2 Turn right onto State Route 116 (Conway Road).

31.2 Keep straight onto SR 116 (South Deerfield Road).

33.2 Keep straight onto SR 116 (Main Street).

33.3 Keep straight onto SR 116 (River Street).

33.8 Bear right onto SR 116 (Ashfield Road).

37.5 Keep straight onto SR 116 (Conway Road).

40.1 Keep straight onto SR 116 (Main Street).

40.5 Turn right onto Buckland Road.

41.3 Turn right onto SR 112 (Ashfield Mountain Road).

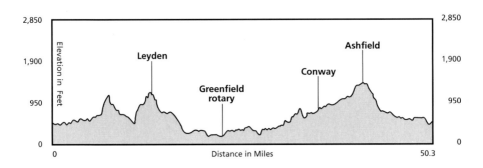

44.4	Turn left onto Upper Street.
45.8	Turn left onto SR 112 (Ashfield Road).
48.9	Turn left onto SR 112 (SR 2).
49.6	Turn right onto SR 112 (Mechanic Street).
49.7	Turn right onto SR 112 (Hope Street), then immediately turn left onto Main Street.
50.1	Turn right onto Water Street.
50.3	Arrive back at start.

Ride Information

Local Information

Shelburne Falls Village Information Center, 75 Bridge Street, Shelburne Falls; (413) 625–2544; www.shelburnefalls.com.

Restaurants

Bakers Country Store, State Route 116, Conway; (413) 369–4936.

Bottle of Bread, 18 Water Street, Shelburne Falls; (413) 625–6502.

Cafe Martin, 24 Bridge Street , Shelburne Falls, (413) 625–2795.

Elmer's Country Store & Deli, 396 Main Street, Ashfield; (413) 628–0188.

Accommodations

Bear Haven B & B, 22 Mechanic Street, Shelburne Falls; (413) 625–9281; www.bear haven.com.

Restrooms

0.1 Shelburne Falls Village Information Center and Shelburne Falls Town Hall

Map

DeLorme Massachusetts Atlas & Gazetteer, pages 22-23.

3 Quabbin Century Classic

Circumnavigate one of the most glorious landmarks in Massachusetts—the Quabbin Reservoir, the source of drinking water for more than half the state's residents. Four towns were "discontinued" to establish the reservoir, which holds 412 billion gallons of drinking water and stretches some 18 miles from north to south. The Quabbin Classic is hilly and challenging, but there are some spectacular views to be enjoyed at the reservoir and a plethora of beautiful quiet country roads to explore and enjoy along your journey to make the effort well worthwhile. The route visits several quaint New England towns, along with the more heavily populated college town of Amherst. Classic town commons, expansive farmlands, stunning water views, challenging climbs, and fast, fun descents make this ride a memorable adventure.

Start: Petersham Memorial Library.
Length: 98.2 miles.
Ride time: 6 to 8 hours.
Terrain: Very, very hilly, with several multimile, steady-grade climbing sections. Also some fantastic, very long descents.

Traffic and hazards: Mostly quiet country roads with only a few miles of busy roads along State Route 9 in Ware and Belchertown and State Route 122 in Petersham. Some rough roads coming back through Orange.

Getting there: State Route 2 West to exit 17/State Route 32—Athol/Petersham. Take a right at the end of the ramp onto SR 32 South and travel for 6 miles. Park along the town common. The library is at 23 Common Street.

From 1928 to 1946 four towns, home to some 2,500 people, were replaced with the Quabbin Reservoir in order to address the need for drinking water that would not require filtration and could be delivered by gravity to Massachusetts's growing population. At the time it was built, the Quabbin Reservoir was the largest man-made reservoir in the world that was dedicated solely to water supply. The Quabbin Classic route will take you completely around the reservoir, with opportunities to take in stunning views of this wonderful site from different perspectives.

Your journey along The Quabbin Classic route will take you through many historic towns. The ride starts in the quaint town common of Petersham, a classic central Massachusetts hill town with a manicured town green, a stunning and unique stone library building, and the requisite white church and town hall. Be sure to visit the general store, where you can get breakfast, lunch, and a variety of supplies.

You'll first descend along State Route 32A, quickly discovering that "numbered routes" carry a distinctly different meaning in the western part of central Massachusetts. As you'll see along this ride, these roads are not heavily traveled, but they are heavily wooded and in great condition. Perfect for cycling.

Just a short way into the route, you'll pass through gate 43 to access a Quabbin

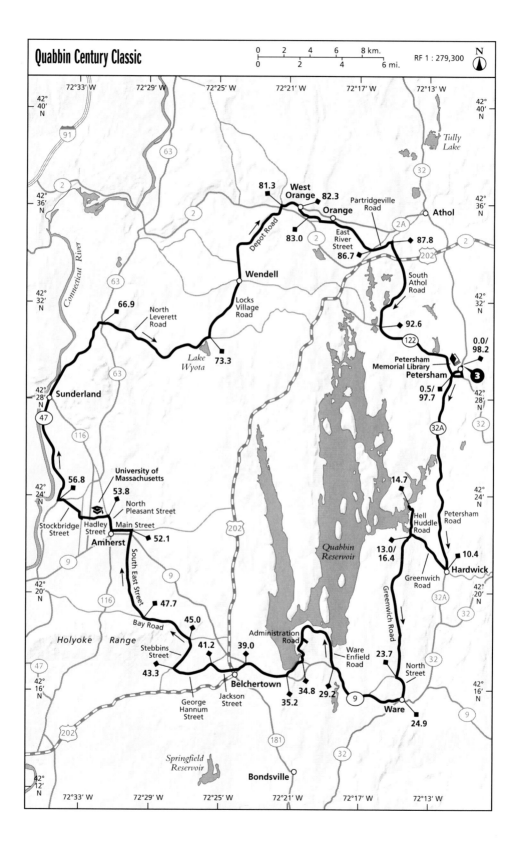

Quabbin Century Classic

0 2 4 6 8 km.

0 2 4 6 mi.

RF 1 : 279,300

N

Reservoir boat ramp. There is a charge for cars but not for bicycles. Ride out to the end to take in some stunning views of the reservoir from water level. Your next vistas of the Quabbin will be quite different, as you view it from various scenic lookout spots on your way up to the lookout tower on Quabbin Hill. Here you'll get a great panoramic view of the reservoir and miles around the surrounding landscape. Be sure to follow the mileage directions carefully as the Ware Enfield Road off of SR 9 is not marked. Also be sure to take care all along SR 9, the busiest road along the route.

Next you'll head over to Belchertown, another hilltop town with an expansive town common and a variety of sources for food and drinks. One of the nice features of these hilltop towns is leaving them—you'll enjoy a great descent out of Belchertown along Jackson Street and especially on George Hannum Street. Just slow down and use caution crossing the railroad tracks on Jackson Street; they are in very bad shape. You will eventually emerge into Amherst, a busy college town with a wide variety of choices for a lunch stop. You'll pass through the University of Massachusetts campus on your way out to State Route 47, a great long stretch of road alongside expansive farmlands. Enjoy the level roads while you can, because you will do a lot of climbing out of Sunderland, through Wendell, and into Orange. Most of that 15-mile stretch is uphill.

Care must be taken in Orange to follow the directions carefully. The roads are also rough and a bit busy. SR 122 offers a respite from the rough road surfaces, but it can be busy and has a narrow shoulder. And, oh yeah, it's a long steady climb all the way along SR 122 back to Petersham!

Miles and Directions

0.0 Depart Petersham Memorial Library.

0.1 Bear right (south) onto SR 32 (South Main Street), then immediately turn right (west) onto SR 32A (Spring Street).

0.5 Bear left (southwest) onto Hardwick Road (SR 32A).

7.2 Road name changes to Petersham Road.

10.4 Turn right (northwest) onto Greenwich Road in the center of Hardwick. Hardwick General Store is across the common.

13.0 Turn right at the sign for gate 43 and take a sharp right onto Hell Huddle Road (not marked). Pass through gate 43 (don't go through gate 43A) and follow the road out to the boat launch area at the end for wonderful views of the Quabbin. Head back out Hell Huddle Road to Greenwich Road.

16.4 Turn right (southwest) onto Greenwich Road.

23.7 Turn left (east) onto North Street, which will take you to the center of Ware.

24.8 Stay on North Street (south).

24.9 Arrive at Ware center. Turn left 1 block for drinks at Ware Package Store or food at Subway. To follow the route, turn right (west) onto SR 9 (SR 32).

29.2 Turn right onto Ware Enfield Road (not marked). Pass through two stone pillars that mark the entrance to the Quabbin Reservoir MDC Reservation. There are two lookouts along the way to the summit tower. Each of the lookouts has portable toilets, but the summit tower does not.

31.1 Road name changes to Administration Road.

32.6 At roundabout, take the second exit onto the summit access road. Enjoy the spectacular panoramic views. Be sure to climb the tower for the full effect.

33.3 Return to the roundabout. At roundabout, take the second exit onto Administration Road.

34.8 Turn right onto Winsor Dam Road. You will need to dismount and go around a gate. This pathway is accessible only to pedestrians and bicycles. You will bike right along the top of the Winsor Dam! Enjoy the spectacular views and tour the visitor center, where there are restrooms. Exit out the visitor center parking lot along Winsor Road.

35.2 Turn right (west) onto SR 9 (Belchertown Road).

39.0 Turn left (south) onto Jabish Street (State Route 21 South). Devon Lane Power Equipment on corner.

39.8 Turn right (north) onto U.S. Route 202 (Main Street). Cold Spring Wine & Spirits has cold drinks and coffee. Little Italy Pizzeria has drinks and food.

40.0 Turn left (west) onto Jackson Street. Caution: You will cross over railroad tracks that are in extremely rough shape.

41.2 Bear left (west) onto George Hannum Street.

43.1 Bear right onto Bachelor Street and follow to end.

43.3 Turn right at stop sign onto Stebbins Street (not marked) and follow to end.

45.0 Turn left at stop sign onto Bay Road (not marked).

47.7 Turn right (north) onto South East Street.

52.1 At first set of lights after crossing SR 9, turn left at stop lights onto Main Street. There's a Subway at 4 Main Street.

53.1 Turn right (north) onto South Pleasant Street.

53.3 Turn left onto North Pleasant Street.

53.8 Go straight at stoplights onto Massachusetts Avenue.

54.4 Road name changes to North Hadley Road.

55.2 Turn right (north) onto Roosevelt Street (not marked).

55.4 Turn left (west) onto Stockbridge Road and follow to end.

56.8 Turn right at stop sign onto SR 47 (River Drive—not marked).

59.4 Keep straight onto SR 47 (Hadley Road).

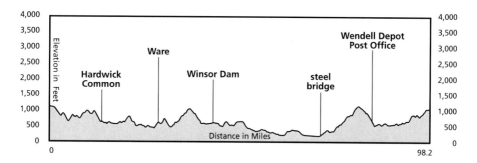

60.1 Keep straight onto SR 47 (River Road).

61.6 Bear left (north) onto SR 47 (South Main Street).

62.1 Keep straight onto SR 47 (North Main Street).

63.5 Keep straight onto SR 47 (Montague Road).

65.9 Keep straight onto SR 47 (Sunderland Road).

66.5 Turn right onto Gunn Road. Cross State Route 63 at stop sign.

66.7 Turn right (east) onto SR 47 (Leverett Road; not marked, but you will immediately pass under a steel bridge).

66.9 Bear left (southeast) onto North Leverett Road.

72.3 Road name changes to Lakeview Road (not marked); follow to end.

73.3 Turn left at stop sign onto Locks Village Road.

76.6 Road name changes to Wendell Depot Road.

81.3 Road name changes to Wendell Road. Turn right immediately after Wendell Depot U.S. Post Office onto West Orange Road (not marked). Caution: Stop sign at bottom of hill.

82.3 Turn right (south) onto Holtshire Road (not marked).

83.0 Turn left (east) onto West River Street and follow it through the town of Orange. The road name changes to East River Street after you cross over Main Street at the lights.

86.4 Road name changes to Partridgeville Road.

86.7 Turn left (northeast) onto Daniel Shays Highway, then immediately bear right (east) onto Partridgeville Road.

87.8 Turn right (south) onto South Athol Road (not marked).

91.8 Road name changes to Meacham Road.

92.6 Keep straight onto SR 122 (Petersham Road).

97.7 Turn left (north) onto SR 32 (South Main Street).

98.1 Bear left (northwest) onto Common Street.

98.2 Arrive back at Petersham Memorial Library.

Ride Information

Local Information
Quabbin Visitor Center, 485 Ware Road (SR 9), Belchertown; (413) 323–7221.

Restaurants
Cold Spring Wine & Spirits, 8 Park Street, Belchertown; (413) 323–7621.

Little Italy, 6 Park Street, Belchertown; (413) 323–0300.

Subway, 52 Main Street, Ware; (413) 967–5022.

Subway, 4 Main Street, Amherst; (413) 256–1919.

Wendell Country Store, 57 Locks Village Road, Wendell; (978) 544–8646.

Accommodations
Winterwood at Petersham Bed & Breakfast, 19 North Main Street, Petersham; (978) 724–8885.

Restrooms
30.2 Enfield Lookout
35.0 Quabbin Visitors Center

Map
DeLorme Massachusetts Atlas & Gazatteer, pages 23, 24-25, 35, 36-37.

4 Petersham Challenge

The Petersham Challenge will take you through the peaceful but steep hills of west-central Massachusetts for a tour of quaint New England hilltop towns to the southeast of the mighty Quabbin Reservoir. You'll visit Barre, North and West Brookfield, and the blink-and-you'll-miss-it New Braintree town center. The ride begins in quiet Petersham, with its inviting town common and convenient general store, which serves a full breakfast and lunch menu. The towns along the route are quaint, and the scenery is stunning, but be prepared for a good workout—the hills are frequent and steep. Fortunately, many great descents can be enjoyed along the route in between the many climbs.

Start: Petersham Memorial Library
Length: 49.5 miles.
Ride time: 3.5 to 4 hours.
Terrain: Very hilly with several long climbs.

Traffic and hazards: Traffic is very light on this route, and shoulders are wide on the busier roads.

Getting there: State Route 2 West to exit 17/State Route 32—Athol/Petersham. Take a right at the end of the ramp onto SR 32 South and follow it for 6 miles. Park along the town common. The Library is at 23 Common Street.

Petersham is a quintessential Massachusetts hilltop town, complete with white church and town hall, quaint town common, and unique stone library. The town is quiet and welcoming and, with its vast natural resources and penchant for outdoor activities, you will feel right at home here on your bike.

The Petersham Challenge takes you to Barre, a small rural community that lies almost exactly in the center of the state. You may be tempted to stop and relax on its large town common, but the ride has just begun and this first segment is by far the easiest of the lot. Don't worry about traveling south along State Route 67 to get to North Brookfield. As you'll soon discover, "numbered routes" have a distinctly different feel in this part of the state. While SR 67 may have more traffic than other roads in the area, the shoulder is wide and the scenery quite enjoyable.

North Brookfield is the most developed of the towns you'll visit along the route, and it may serve as a good lunch spot, being just under the route's halfway point. North Brookfield's development is a testament to its rich history of being successful not only in farming but also in industry, primarily in shoe manufacturing and rubber. The town's ingenuity was further rewarded by its ability to avoid the smallpox epidemic of the 1770s by taking the innovative step of inoculating its 200 residents with an experimental vaccine. North Brookfield is also the home of famous major league baseball manager Connie Mack, who won five World Series crowns.

New Braintree offers a distinctly different appeal in its size and simplicity. If you don't pay careful attention, you may miss the town center altogether. However, you

North Brookfield Luncheonette

won't forget your ride down Wine Road out of the town center. It's a roller coaster of steep climbs and descents that will be sure to make an impression, and you'll want to use extra care on the descents, some of which are over rough pavement with limited visibility.

Gilbertsville represents your last chance to stop for snacks and drinks before embarking on the long and enjoyable ride up State Route 32A back into Petersham. For a peek at the Quabbin Reservoir, you can add a few miles to the ride with a jaunt up Greenwich Road. Enter at gate 43 and take a ride out to the water along Hell Huddle Road.

Miles and Directions

0.0   Depart Petersham Memorial Library.

0.1   Turn left onto West Street. Road name changes to East Street.

3.3   Road name changes to Old Barre Road (not marked).

4.4   Road name changes to Pleasant Street (not marked). Follow into Barre center.

7.6   Departing Barre center, bear left onto State Route 122 South (SR 32).

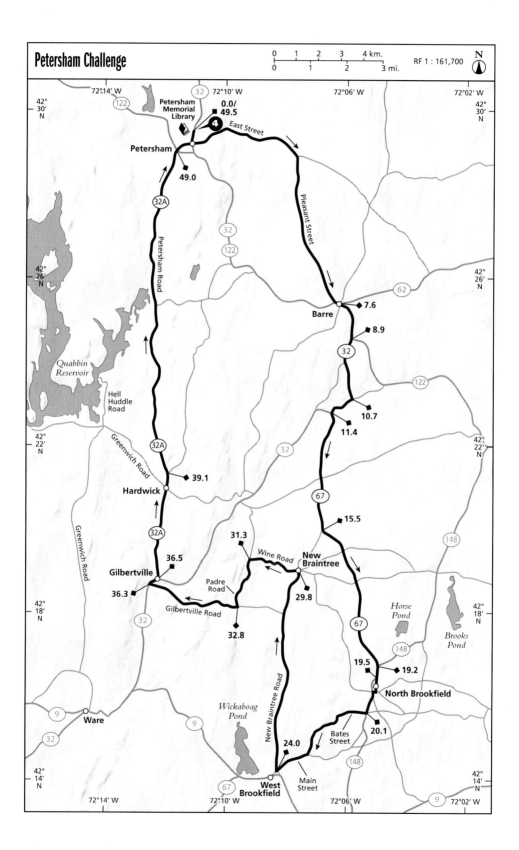

Petersham Challenge

0   1   2   3   4 km.

0   1   2   3 mi.

RF 1 : 161,700

N

8.9 Keep right onto SR 32 (South Barre Road).

9.2 Keep right to stay on SR 32 (South Barre Road).

10.7 Turn right onto SR 32 (Main Street).

11.4 Turn right onto SR 32 (Wheelwright Road), then immediately turn left onto SR 67 (North Brookfield Road).

13.4 Keep straight onto SR 67 (Barre Road).

15.5 Turn left to stay on SR 67 (Barre Road).

19.2 Bear right onto State Route 148 (SR 67).

19.5 Bear left onto Grove Street.

19.9 Turn right onto School Street, then immediately turn left onto SR 148 (SR 67).

20.1 Turn right onto SR 67.

21.0 Keep straight onto SR 67 (West Brookfield Road).

22.8 Keep straight onto SR 67 (North Main Street).

24.0 Turn right onto Church Street, then immediately right again onto New Braintree Road.

27.2 Road name changes to West Brookfield Road.

29.8 Turn left onto Wine Road. Caution: Wine Road has steep climbs and also very steep descents, some with rough pavement and limited visibility.

31.3 Turn left onto West Road.

32.0 Turn right onto Padre Road.

32.8 Turn right onto Gilbertville Road.

36.2 Road name changes to New Braintree Road.

36.3 Turn right onto SR 32 (Main Street).

36.5 Bear left onto SR 32A (Hardwick Road).

39.1 Bear left onto SR 32A (Petersham Road).

44.4 Bear left onto SR 32A (Hardwick Road).

49.0 Bear right onto SR 32A (South Main Street).

49.3 Turn left onto SR 32 (South Main Street), then immediately bear left onto Common Street.

49.5 Arrive back at Petersham Memorial Library.

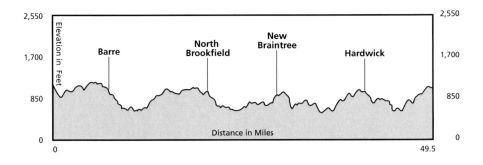

Ride Information

Local Information

Central Massachusetts Tourist Council,
30 Worcester Center Boulevard, Worcester;
www.worcester.org.

Restaurants

Country Store, 2 North Main Street, Petersham, (978) 724-3245.
North Brookfield Country Kitchen, 37 Grove Street, North Brookfield.

Accommodations

Winterwood at Petersham, 19 North Main Street , Petersham; (978) 724-8885.

Map

DeLorme Massachusetts Atlas & Gazetteer, pages 36-37.

5 Princeton Challenge

Beginning in Lancaster and passing through a gauntlet of hills at the Sterling-Leominster border, the majority of the Princeton Challenge route is a wonderful tour of the back roads surrounding Wachusett Mountain. Farmland and thick forests dominate the landscape, along with many water views at various reservoirs and ponds along the way. But make no mistake, this route is for hill climbers and others who enjoy challenging climbs and fun and fast descents on quiet, low-traffic roads.

Start: Downtown Lancaster in front of Atlantic Union College.
Length: 66.3 miles.
Ride time: 4.5 to 5 hours.
Terrain: Very hilly.

Traffic and hazards: Short stretch along State Route 68 has busy traffic but also a wide shoulder. Some descents require extra caution, as noted in the Miles and Directions section.

Getting there: From Interstate 495 South, take exit 27 to State Route 117 West. Follow for 3 miles and turn left onto State Route 110 South. Follow to State Route 70/Main Street. There's on-street parking along Main Street.

The Princeton Challenge is a tough route with limited food and water stops. Be sure that you're in good shape and well-prepared before heading out on this one. Also be sure to pay close attention to mileage on the directions, as many of the streets are not marked.

Based on the popular Grand View ride run by the Charles River Wheelmen, the Princeton Challenge will test your climbing legs along a breathtaking backdrop of scenic country roads. From Lancaster Center, you'll enter Sterling near its famous Davis' Farmland attraction. A popular family spot, Davis' Farmland is a seventh-generation family farm that offers a great petting zoo for younger children in the spring, a water

Riders on Wachusett Street in Leominster

spray-ground in the summer, and apple picking in the fall. Directly across the street is Davis' MegaMaze, a challenging field-maze adventure for older children and adults.

From Sterling Center, you'll climb up through Leominster's scenic back roads, climbing past the former site of the Grand View Country Club, a hilltop vista where the original Charles River Wheelmen route derived its name.

The loop through Princeton begins by heading south through sparsely populated roads along the Trout Brook and Quinapoxet Reservations to the farmlands along the Holden and Rutland borders, before emerging in Princeton's town center. Incorporated in 1759, Princeton was named after the Rev. Thomas Prince, pastor of the Old South Church in Boston, and one of the first proprietors of the town. His son-in-law, Moses Gill, would later become governor of Massachusetts. The town's biggest attraction today, no doubt, is Wachusett Mountain State Reservation and its popular ski resort. During spring and summer, cyclists enjoy climbing the mountain, and each July it serves as a centerpiece of the Fitchburg-Lonsjo classic stage race, which attracts professional and amateur racers from all over the country. The Princeton Challenge route skips the summit climb, but you can easily add it in if you are feeling ambitious.

As you head back through East Princeton and Sterling, you may be tempted to exert a sigh of relief. Not so fast—the toughest climb is yet to come. Ascending Justice Hill Road is easily the toughest climb of the day, so be sure to save some energy for the last part of the route.

Miles and Directions

0.0   Depart 272 Main Street, Lancaster, onto SR 70 (Main Street).

0.2   Turn left onto George Hill Road.

0.5   Bear left onto Goss Lane.

1.4   Turn right onto Sterling Road.

1.5   Keep straight onto Deershorn Road.

2.2   Turn right onto State Route 62 (Sterling Street).

2.3   Turn left onto Redstone Hill Road.

3.4   Turn left onto Rugg Road.

4.0   Turn right onto Maple Street (marked, but easy to miss).

5.3   Turn right onto State Route 12 (SR 62), then immediately turn left onto Park Street (not marked) around the small town common.

5.4   Turn right onto Meetinghouse Hill Road.

5.7   Keep straight onto Rowley Hill Road.

6.1   Keep right onto Tuttle Road.

6.3   Keep right to stay on Tuttle Road.

8.0   Turn right onto Heywood Road (not marked).

9.6   Road name changes to Pleasant Street.

10.7 Turn left onto Wachusett Street. Caution: There are some rough patches of pavement on the downhill side of Wachusett Street.

13.5 Road name changes to Hastings Road.

13.8 Turn right onto Justice Hill Road (sharp right) Caution: Steep downhill with a sharp left turn at the bottom.

14.0 Turn left onto Lucas Road.

14.5 Bear right onto Justice Hill Cutoff.

14.8 Road name changes to Leominster Road.

15.2 Turn right onto State Route 140 (Main Street).

15.5 Stop at Quick Stop Convenience Store, then turn left out of parking lot and reverse dirction back down SR 140.

15.6 Turn right onto Gleason Road.

16.8 Turn right onto Houghton Road (not marked).

16.9 Turn left onto Bullard Road (not marked).

17.9 Turn right onto SR 62, then immediately turn left onto Coalkiln Road.

19.7 Road name changes to Mason Road.

22.0 Bear left onto State Route 31 (Wachusett Street—not marked).

Princeton Challenge

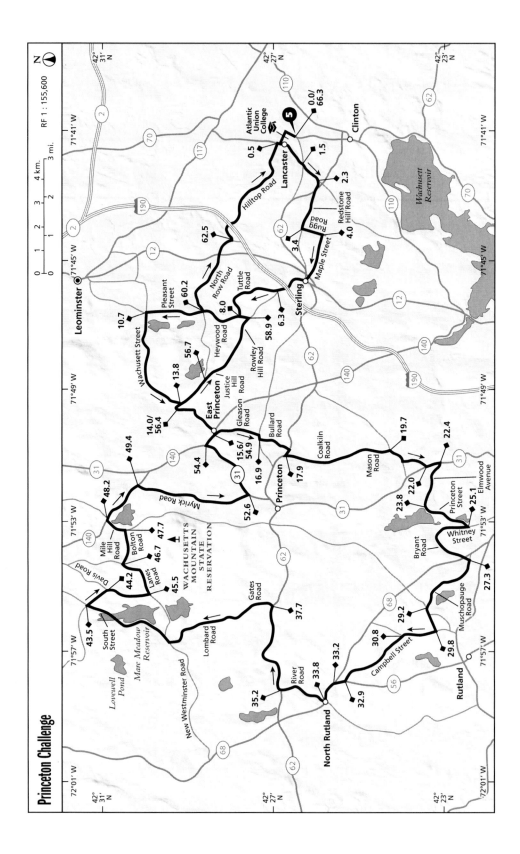

RF 1 : 155,600

22.4	Turn right onto Elmwood Avenue.
23.8	Bear left onto Princeton Street (not marked).
25.1	Turn right onto Whitney Street (hairpin turn up a steep hill).
25.9	Road name changes to Bryant Road.
27.2	Road name changes to Parsons Road.
27.3	Turn right onto Muschopauge Road (not marked).
28.0	Turn right to remain on Muschopauge Road.
29.2	Bear left onto Wachusett Street (not marked).
29.8	Turn right onto Glenwood Road (not marked).
30.8	Bear left onto Campbell Street.
32.9	Turn right onto State Route 56 (Pomagusset Road—not marked).
33.2	Turn left onto State Route 68 (East County Road). Caution: Very busy road, but it does have a wide shoulder.
33.8	Turn right onto River Road. Note: Food and water can be had at Town Line Variety just beyond this intersection on the other side of SR 68 (you can see it from this corner).
34.9	Road name changes to Upper Intervale Road.
35.2	Bear right onto SR 62 (Old Boston Turnpike—not marked). Caution: Busy road, but an ample shoulder.
36.4	Bear right to remain on SR 62 (Hubbardston Road). Caution: Watch for railroad tracks at end before turning onto Gates Road.
37.7	Turn left onto Gates Road.
39.0	Road name changes to Lombard Road. Caution: Some rough pavement.
40.9	Turn right onto New Westminster Road (not marked).
41.8	Road name changes to South Street.
43.5	Turn right onto Harrington Road.
44.2	Bear right onto Davis Road.
45.5	Turn left onto Lanes Road.
46.2	Bear left onto West Princeton Road.
46.7	Turn right onto Bolton Road. Great, enjoyable stairstep descent. Enjoy it but use caution— at the very bottom is a stop sign.
47.7	Bear left onto Mile Hill Road.
48.2	Turn right onto SR 140 (Worcester Road).

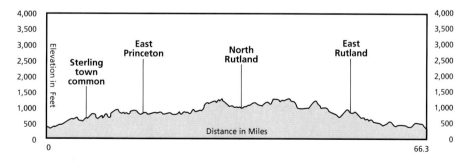

49.4	Turn right onto Myrick Road.
51.3	Turn left to stay on Myrick Road.
52.6	Turn left onto SR 31 (East Princeton Road–not marked).
54.4	Bear right onto SR 140 (Main Street).
54.7	Pass Quick Stop Convenience Store again.
54.9	Turn left onto Leominster Road.
55.4	Road name changes to Justice Hill Cutoff. Toughest climb of the ride.
56.4	Bear right onto Justice Hill Road. Caution: Fast descent, but you need to turn left at the bottom.
56.7	Bear left onto Upper North Row Road.
56.8	Turn left onto Justice Hill Road.
58.4	Road name changes to Rowley Hill Road.
58.9	Turn left onto Heywood Road.
60.2	Bear right onto North Row Road.
61.9	Road name changes to Pratts Junction Road.
62.5	Turn left onto Flanagan Hill Road.
63.8	Road name changes to Hilltop Road.
64.9	Bear left onto George Hill Road.
65.7	Bear right to stay on George Hill Road.
65.8	Bear left to stay on George Hill Road.
66.1	Turn right onto SR 70 (Main Street).
66.3	Arrive back at 272 Main Street.

Ride Information

Local Information

Central Massachusetts Tourist Council, 30 Worcester Center Boulevard, Worcester; www.worcester.org.

Local Events and Attractions

Fitchburg Longsjo Classic Bicycle Stage Race, P.O. Box 923, Fitchburg, MA 01420; (978) 534-9966; www.longsjo.com. July Fourth weekend.
Wachusett Mountain, 499 Mountain Road, Princeton; (978) 464-2300; www.wachusett.com.

Restaurants

Michael's Bridge Diner, 57 Main Street, Lancaster; (978) 368-0630.

Accommodations

Wachusett Mountain, 499 Mountain Road, Princeton; (978) 464-2300; www.wachusett.com.

Map

DeLorme Massachusetts Atlas & Gazetteer, pages 25, 26, 37, 38.

6 Mount Wachusett Classic

This is no mere century ride—it's an epic journey through central Massachusetts from historic Concord to peaceful Princeton. At Princeton, solid rock juts 2,000 feet toward the sky to form Mount Wachusett, a great family spot for skiing in the winter that also provides a challenging climb for cyclists throughout the rest of the year. A quick glance at the course profile will show you that this isn't the only climb along the route. Pack well, be sure you're fit, and embark on a classic cycling adventure based on the very popular and aptly named Climb to the Clouds ride run annually by the Charles River Wheelmen.

Start: Thoreau Street, Concord.
Length: 102.1 miles.
Ride time: 6 to 8 hours.
Terrain: Very hilly with a mountain summit climb.

Traffic and hazards: Along the route are mostly low-traffic roads or roads that offer wide shoulders. Care must be taken crossing a couple of major roads and when riding along State Route 117 and State Route 140, as each is a busy road with a narrow shoulder.

Getting there: On-street public parking is available along tennis courts on Thoreau Street. If all the spots are taken, you can park around the corner on the side of the tennis courts on Everett Street.

Concord's rich history makes this a great ride to plan for an overnight stay. There are a plethora of wonderful sites to enjoy, such as the Old North Bridge, site of the "shot hear around the world," Walden Pond Reservation, and homes and artifacts from such famous revolutionaries as Henry David Thoreau, Ralph Waldo Emerson, Nathaniel Hawthorne, and Louisa May Alcott. There are also lots of shops and eateries in the center of town, and a great museum, the Concord Museum on Lexington Road, which is probably the best place to start any historical tour of the area.

There are ample stops along the way to refuel, but make no mistake—you're in for a long haul. Be sure to start out with some energy bars in your pocket and a couple of large water bottles filled with your favorite drink as you head out on this classic cycling journey through central Massachusetts.

This epic cycling adventure is based on the very popular Climb to the Clouds ride run annually by the largest recreational cycling club in the state, the Charles River Wheelmen. The ride will wind its way out through the hilly country roads of Sudbury, Bolton, and Lancaster before kicking up a notch further in Sterling and on to the big climb itself. At the very beginning of the ride, you'll pass Walden Pond Reservation, considered the birthplace of the conservation movement. This is where Henry David Thoreau lived in a cabin from 1845 to 1847, an experience that inspired his famous book *Walden,* which helped to inspire respect for the natural environment. Historic sites fade into winding country roads as you head toward this ride's big challenge: climbing to the summit of Mount Wachusett.

Mount Wachusett Classic

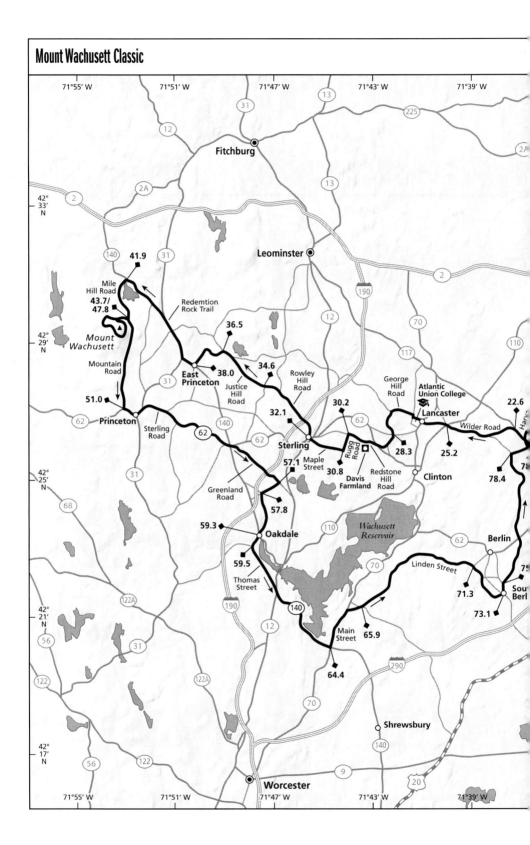

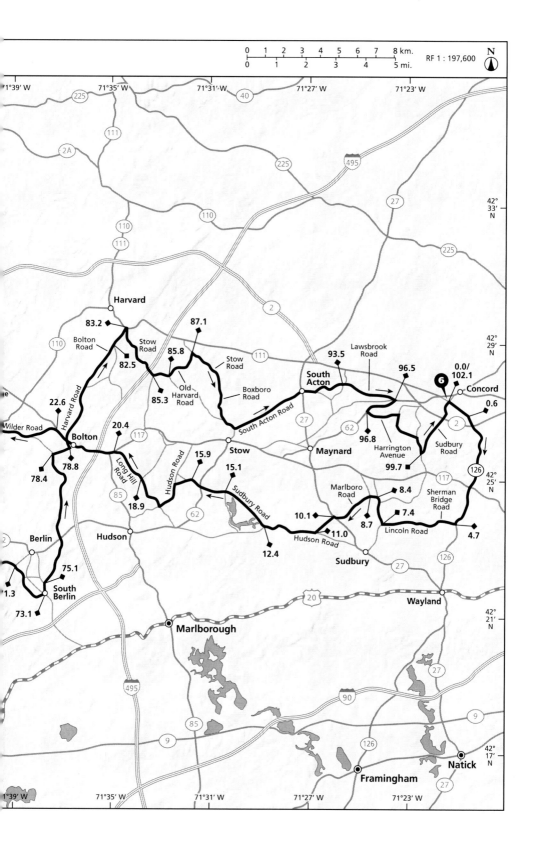

Mount Wachusett has a rich history with the sport of cycling. It is a key fixture of the annual Fitchburg-Lonsjo Classic, which began as a road race in memory of Art Lonsjo in 1960 after his tragic death at the age of twenty-six and has since evolved into a prominent national stage race. Art Lonsjo was a world-class speed skater who also took up cycling. He is probably best known for the rare accomplishment of competing in both the winter and summer Olympic games in the same year (1956). Mount Wachusett formed the basis for one of his regular training routes and subsequently the race that took on his name. Many top cyclists have competed at the event, including Lance Armstrong, Greg LeMond, Tyler Hamilton, Connie Carpenter, and Davis Phinney.

The toughest part of the climb is the 1-mile ascent up Mile Hill Road, which has an average grade of about 9 percent. You can catch your breath at the visitor center, which has restrooms and an outdoor drinking water fountain, before going up the summit road. On a clear day you can see Boston from the summit; a cloudy day may offer a true opportunity to "climb to the clouds." Regardless of the weather, use extreme caution on the descent. It is very rough pavement and very steep. Go slowly.

With the mountain climb behind you, you'll have a chance to enjoy quite a bit of downhill riding before the climbs start again. You'll sweep around Wachusett Reservoir on your way to the very quiet, winding country roads of Berlin—some of the best riding roads in the state. With most of the ride under your belt, you may want to indulge yourself in an ice cream at the quaint Berlin Orchards Store. Go ahead and enjoy—there are still a couple of steep climbs to conquer on the way back.

Miles and Directions

0.0 Depart 251 Thoreau Street and head east.

0.6 Bear right (south) onto Walden Street.

0.9 Road name changes to State Route 126 (Walden Street).

4.7 Turn right (west) onto Sherman Bridge Road.

5.5 Road name changes to Lincoln Road.

7.4 Turn right (north) onto Concord Road.

8.2 Keep straight onto Pantry Road.

8.4 Bear left (west) onto Haynes Road.

8.7 Turn left (south) onto Marlboro Road.

10.1 Bear right (west) onto State Route 27 (Maynard Road—not marked), then immediately turn left (southwest) onto Fairbank Road.

11.0 Bear right (west) onto Hudson Road.

12.4 Road name changes to Sudbury Road.

15.1 Bear right (west) onto Boon Road.

15.8 Bear right (north) onto Randall Road (not marked).

15.9 Turn left to stay on Randall Road (not marked), and pass by Stow Acres Country Club golf course.

16.7 Bear left (southwest) onto Hudson Road (not marked).

17.3 Road name changes to Zina Road.

17.4 Bear right (west) onto Old Stow Road (not marked).

17.7 Turn right (north) onto Old Bolton Road.

18.5 Road name changes to Woobly Road.

18.9 Keep straight onto Long Hill Road.

20.4 Turn left (west) onto SR 117 (Main Street—not marked), a busy road with a narrow shoulder.

21.0 Country Cupboard Convenience Store.

22.6 Keep left onto Wilder Road (follow sign for Twin Springs golf course).

24.5 Road name changes to Old Common Road.

25.2 Bear left (west) onto Bolton Road (sign is hard to see).

25.9 Keep right onto George Hill Road (sign is hard to see).

26.5 Bear left (west) onto George Hill Road.

28.2 Bear left (east) onto Sterling Road.

28.3 Turn right (west) onto Deershorn Road.

29.0 Turn right (northwest) onto State Route 62 (Sterling Street).

29.1 Turn left (southwest) onto Redstone Hill Road.

30.2 Turn left (south) onto Rugg Road.

30.8 Turn right (west) onto Maple Street (not marked).

32.1 Turn right (east) onto State Route 12 (SR 62), then immediately turn left (northwest) onto Park Street.

32.2 Turn right (north) onto Meetinghouse Hill Road.

32.5 Keep straight onto Rowley Hill Road.

34.6 Road name changes to Justice Hill Road.

36.5 Keep left onto Justice Hill Cutoff.

36.6 Keep left to stay on Justice Hill Cutoff.

37.5 Road name changes to Leominster Road.

38.0 Turn right (west) onto SR 140 (Main Street).

38.1 Quick Stop Convenience Store.

41.9 Turn left (south) onto Mile Hill Road.

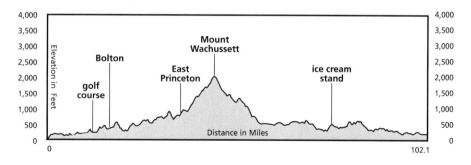

42.9 Road name changes to Mountain Road.

43.7 Turn right (west) onto access road, Wachusett Mountian State Reservation Visitor Center entrance.

45.9 Turn left (north) onto access road.

46.1 Wachusett Mountain summit.

46.2 Turn left (east) onto access road as you leave the summit.

47.1 Turn right (east) at stop sign onto access road.

47.8 Turn right (southeast) out of the visitor center onto Mountain Road.

51.0 Turn left (east) onto State Route 31 (SR 62).

51.5 Road name changes to SR 62 (Sterling Road).

54.6 Keep straight onto SR 62 (Princeton Road).

55.1 Bear right (east) onto Greenland Road (not marked).

56.8 Bear right (southeast) onto Boutelle Road.

57.1 Turn right (south) onto Muddy Pond Road.

57.8 Bear left (south) onto John Dee Road.

58.7 Road name changes to Washacum Street.

59.3 Bear left (south) onto SR 140 (North Main Street).

59.5 Keep straight onto Thomas Street.

60.7 Bear left (southeast) onto Crescent Street.

61.1 Road name changes to Central Street.

61.5 Road name changes to SR 140 (Worcester Street).

61.6 Honey Farms Convenience Store.

64.4 Turn left (north) onto State Route 70 (Main Street).

65.7 Boylston Center Store, center of Boylston, nice little town green.

65.9 Turn right (east) onto Central Street (not marked).

66.4 Bear left (northeast) onto Linden Street.

71.3 Turn right (south) onto Crosby Road.

73.1 Turn left (north) onto Pleasant Street.

73.4 Keep right onto Sawyer Hill Road. Caution: Stop sign at bottom of steep hill.

75.1 Turn left (west) onto SR 62 (Central Street), then immediately turn right (north) onto Sawyer Hill Road.

75.2 Berlin Orchards Store & Ice Cream Stand.

76.3 Road name changes to Frye Road.

76.7 Keep straight onto Berlin Road (not marked).

78.4 Bear right (east) onto Wattaquadock Road (not marked), then immediately turn left (north) onto Manor Road.

78.8 Road name changes to Harvard Road.

81.0 Road name changes to Bolton Road.

82.5 Bear right (northeast) onto Slough Road. Caution: Dangerous intersection, stop sign at bottom of hill.

83.2 Turn right (southeast) onto Stow Road. Hairpin right turn.

85.3	Turn left (east) onto Eldridge Road.
85.8	Turn left (northeast) onto Old Harvard Road (not marked).
87.1	Turn right (southeast) onto Burroughs Road (not marked).
87.8	Bear right (east) at stop sign onto Chester Road (not marked).
88.0	Bear right (south) at stop sign onto Stow Road (not marked).
88.6	Road name changes to Boxboro Road.
90.5	Road name changes to South Acton Road.
92.1	Road name changes to Stow Street.
92.8	Turn left at stop sign (northwest) onto Martin Street (not marked, pass by baseball field on your right).
93.1	Turn right (east) onto Central Street.
93.4	Keep straight onto SR 27 (Main Street).
93.5	Turn left (east) onto School Street.
95.3	Keep straight onto Lawsbrook Road (not marked).
95.8	Road name changes to Laws Brook Road.
95.9	Bear right (south) onto Hillside Avenue.
96.2	Turn left (east) onto Old Stow Road.
96.5	Turn right (west) at stop sign onto SR 62 (Main Street—not marked).
96.8	Turn left (southeast) onto Harrington Avenue.
97.0	Bear left to remain on Harrington Avenue (not marked).
98.0	Turn right (south) at stop sign onto Old Marlboro Road (not marked).
98.3	Turn left (south) onto Williams Road.
99.2	Bear right (south) at stop sign onto Old Road To Nine Acre Corner (not marked).
99.7	Turn left (north) onto Sudbury Road.
101.8	Turn right (southeast) onto Thoreau Street.
102.1	Arrive back at 251 Thoreau Street.

Ride Information

Local Information

Central Massachusetts Tourist Council, 30 Worcester Center Boulevard, Worcester; www.worcester.org.

Concord Museum, 200 Lexington Road, Concord; (978) 369-9763.

Local Events and Attractions

Fitchburg Longsjo Classic Bicycle Stage Race, (978) 534-9966; www.longsjo.com. July Fourth weekend.

Wachusett Mountain, 499 Mountain Road, Princeton; (978) 464-2300; www.wachusett.com.

Restaurants

Papa Gino's, 195 Sudbury Road, Concord; (978) 369-0561.

Accommodations

Best Western at Historic Concord, 740 Elm Street, Concord; (978) 369-6100.

Concord's Colonial Inn, 48 Monument Square, Concord; (800) 370-9200, (978) 369-9200.

Map

DeLorme Massachusetts Atlas & Gazetteer, pages 26, 37, 38-39, 40

7 Lunenburg Cruise

Most of the Lunenburg Cruise is over flat roads or rolling hills, a rare treat for central Massachusetts riding. You will need to conquer a couple of long climbs and a few short, steep hills, but mostly you will be enjoying long stretches on tree-lined back roads with little traffic, occasional water views of small lakes and dammed rivers, and three town centers with a variety of quaint historic buildings. A brief excursion into southern New Hampshire, passing through expansive open lands, nicely rounds out the ride.

Start: Downtown Lunenburg across from the Ritter Memorial Library.
Length: 41 miles.
Ride time: 2.5 to 3.0 hours.
Terrain: A long ride on mostly low-traffic, tree-lined country roads with many rolling hills, two long climbs, and some short, steep hills.

Traffic and hazards: Most of the route is on fairly isolated roads, with few houses and cars. Care must be taken on some sections that, though somewhat isolated from traffic, are narrow and winding with limited visibility on corners and up or down hills. Some shorter sections are on busy roads or cross over busy roads.

Getting there: From east or west, take State Route 2 to State Route 13 north for 4.3 miles. Turn right onto State Route 2A/Massachusetts Avenue and travel 1.8 miles to the intersection of Main Street. The fire station and library will be on your right. Free parking is abundant along Main Street. There is also public parking in a lot between the Congregational Church and the Chester Mossman Youth Center off Memorial Drive.

The ride starts in the center of Lunenburg, a wonderfully approachable Massachusetts small town center composed primarily of a library, town hall, and church spread across the top of a commanding hill at the intersection of Massachusetts Avenue and Main Street. You'll clip in and roll a short way down SR 2A, one of the few busy roads in the area, before escaping to the placid Hickory Hills Lake area. Here you begin winding down country roads with expansive lake views on your left as the houses begin to get farther and farther apart and the trees start to dominate the landscape.

Though there'll be no sign that you've moved on, you'll quickly pass into Townsend and enjoy some of its gently rolling country roads. The peace and quiet is only briefly interrupted in order to cross the busy State Route 119 at a traffic light and head into Pepperell, where the hills become a little more pronounced and the scenery more heavily wooded in areas.

About 12 miles into the ride, you will cross the New Hampshire border and begin to enjoy the hills of West Hollis. Here's where you'll begin your first real uphill section of the ride. This effort will be well rewarded with a nice flat run on Twiss Lane where large sections of the road are framed by open farmlands.

Squannacook River Dam, West Groton

At just about the halfway point, downtown Dunstable emerges. Dunstable is a modest and quiet town of 17 square miles of sparsely populated countryside, plenty of room for its 2,800 residents, but quite a bit smaller than the 200 square miles it occupied in 1673 when it was originally incorporated.

The Convenient Mann, a great stop for refreshments where you can get anything from a bottle of sports drink to a full lunch from their deli, is in the town center along Pleasant Street just after the intersection with Main Street. Tables are available inside or you can cross the street and spread out on the lawn of the Swallow Union Elementary School.

The next section of the ride goes most of the way around the edge of Massapoag Pond on a great winding road with rolling hills and wonderful water views. Here the traffic is very light, but care must be taken as the road gets narrow at points and visibility is limited on some sharp corners.

As you round the corner on Island Pond Road and begin to head away from the pond, you'll begin a short, steep climb up to Old Dunstable Road and a great long section of rolling hills on good pavement that heads into Groton. Downtown Groton offers an array of services and shops for just about anything you may need. There

Lunenburg Cruise

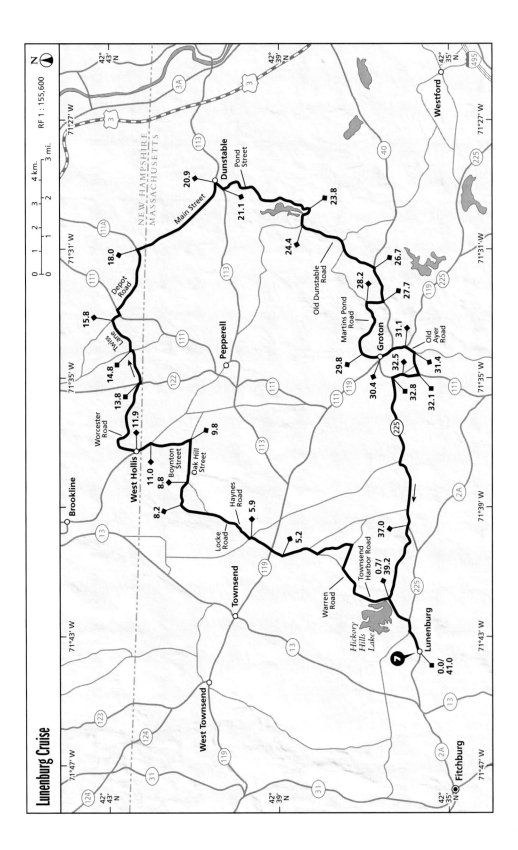

RF 1 : 155,600

are also many great historical buildings along Main Street, such as the Governor Boutwell House, built in 1851, which is the current home of the Groton Historical Society Museum (admission is free, but the museum is open by appointment only). A great resting spot is on the expansive lawn of the First Parish Church, also on Main Street. The Groton Minutemen assembled on this very spot before heading to Concord and Lexington to battle the British in the Revolutionary War. The church's iron bell was cast by the Paul Revere Foundry, an iron and brass foundry established by the famous patriot in 1787.

As you head out of Groton, you'll end up on a long section of State Route 225, which offers a great sweeping downhill section but also includes your second mile-plus uphill riding section of the route. Though the shoulders are wide, SR 225 is also a fairly busy road. Be careful.

A few miles later you will dart off down Mulpus Road, which will lead you back to Hickory Hills Lake and eventually back to downtown Lunenburg.

Miles and Directions

0.0 Start at Lunenburg center, at the intersection of SR 2A and Main Street. Head west on SR 2A, traveling downhill by Lunenburg High School. Use caution as this can be a busy road, and it has a narrow shoulder.

0.7 Turn left onto Townsend Harbor Road, passing by Hickory Hills Lake on the left. Follow the perimeter of the lake, bearing left to remain on Townsend Harbor Road.

2.0 Bear right at fork to stay on Townsend Harbor Road.

2.6 Townsend Harbor Road becomes Warren Road as you enter Townsend.

5.2 Bear right onto South Street.

5.3 At intersection, proceed straight across SR 119 to Spaulding Street.

5.9 Turn left onto Wallace Hill Road.

6.0 Turn right onto Haynes Road.

7.2 Haynes Road becomes Locke Road (not marked).

7.8 Locke Road becomes Wheeler Street (not marked).

8.2 Turn right onto Cranberry Street (not marked).

8.8 Bear left onto Chestnut Street.

9.0 Bear left onto Oak Hill Street.

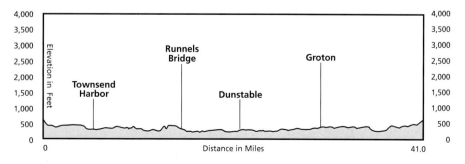

9.8 Turn left onto Boynton Street.

11.0 At end of Boynton Street, turn left onto Brookline Street (not marked).

11.5 Turn right onto Worcester Road (not marked, old barn at intersection).

11.9 Bear right, remaining on Worcester Road.

13.8 Turn right at stop sign at end of road onto State Route 122. Caution: SR 122 is a busy road.

13.9 Turn left onto Blood Road (not marked, stone wall).

14.7 Turn left onto Dow Road (not marked).

14.8 Turn right onto Twiss Lane.

15.8 At the end of Twiss Lane, turn right at stop sign onto Depot Road. Caution: Depot Road is a busy road with no shoulder.

16.1 Turn left onto Runnells Bridge Road (which is also State Route 111 East). Caution: Busy road.

16.2 Turn right at lights onto Depot Road (not marked).

18.0 Turn right onto Gregg Road.

18.3 Gregg Road becomes Main Street.

20.9 Turn right at stop sign onto Pleasant Street (State Route 113 West).

21.0 Convenient Mann convenience store/deli.

21.1 Turn left onto Pond Street at bottom of hill.

21.7 Bear left, remaining on Pond Street.

23.8 Turn right at stop sign onto Groton Road.

23.9 Groton Road becomes Island Pond Road.

24.4 Turn left onto Old Dunstable Road.

26.7 Turn right at stop sign onto Lowell Road (not marked). Caution: Busy road.

27.7 Turn right onto School House Road.

28.2 Turn left at stop sign onto Martins Pond Road.

29.8 Turn left at stop sign onto Hollis Street (not marked).

30.4 Turn left onto Main Street.

30.6 Dunkin' Donuts coffee shop.

31.0 Cumberland Farms convenience store.

31.1 Turn right onto Old Ayer Road.

31.4 Turn right onto Peabody Street.

32.1 Turn right onto Higley Street.

32.5 Turn right onto Farmers Row.

32.8 Turn left onto SR 225.

35.2 Turn left at lights, remaining on SR 225.

37.0 Turn right onto Mulpus Road.

39.2 Turn left onto Townsend Harbor Road.

40.1 Turn right onto Massachusetts Avenue/SR 2A. Caution: Busy road with a narrow shoulder on this side.

41.0 Arrive back at center of Lunenberg.

Ride Information

Local Information

Central Massachusetts Tourist Council, 30 Worcester Center Boulevard, Worcester; www.worcester.org.

Restaurants

Centre Pizza Restaurant, 1353 Massachusetts Avenue, Lunenburg; (978) 582-9876.

Accommodations

The Harley House, 909 Massachusetts Avenue, Lunenburg; (978) 582-9421.

Restrooms

0.0 Ritter Memorial Library

21.0 Convenient Mann grocery/deli

Map

DeLorme Massachusetts Atlas & Gazetteer, pages 26-27.

8 Souhegan River Classic

Based on the popular Fall Century Ride of the Charles River Wheelmen, the Souhegan River Classic is a challenging century—virtually all of the route's 5,500 feet of climbing are crammed into the first 62 miles. Painful, but beautiful, the Souhegan River Classic takes you through the best cycling roads of northcentral Massachusetts to the best cycling roads of southcentral New Hampshire. Be sure that you are in good shape and pack well, as food and water stops are few and far between.

Start: Acton Memorial Library, Acton.
Length: 100.4 miles.
Ride time: 6 to 7 hours.

Terrain: Very hilly. Several long, challenging climbs.
Traffic and hazards: Virtually the entire route is on low-traffic back roads.

Getting there: Take State Route 2 East to exit 42/State Route 27 North. Follow for 1 mile to the library, and park around the back in the parking lot.

A century ride can be challenging. A very hilly metric-century can be equally challenging. The Souhegan River Classic will take you on a journey of both. You'll climb your way from the quaint rural town of Acton, inside the Interstate 495 beltway, all the way up through the scenic hills alongside the Souhegan River in southern New Hampshire, completing a very hilly metric century ride just before re-entering Massachusetts. You'll complete the ride along wonderful Massachusetts back roads that wind all the way back to Acton.

Though located just 25 miles from Boston, Acton is a quiet rural New England town with a classic town center. You'll enjoy a comfortable cruise most of the way to Groton before you start climbing your way along State Route 225 and eventually into Lunenburg, where the hills become challenging and the views more expansive.

Soughegan River Classic

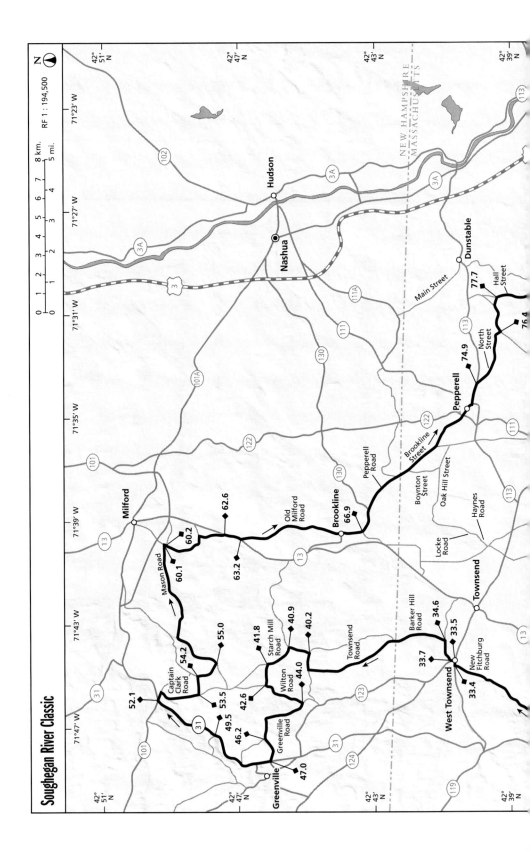

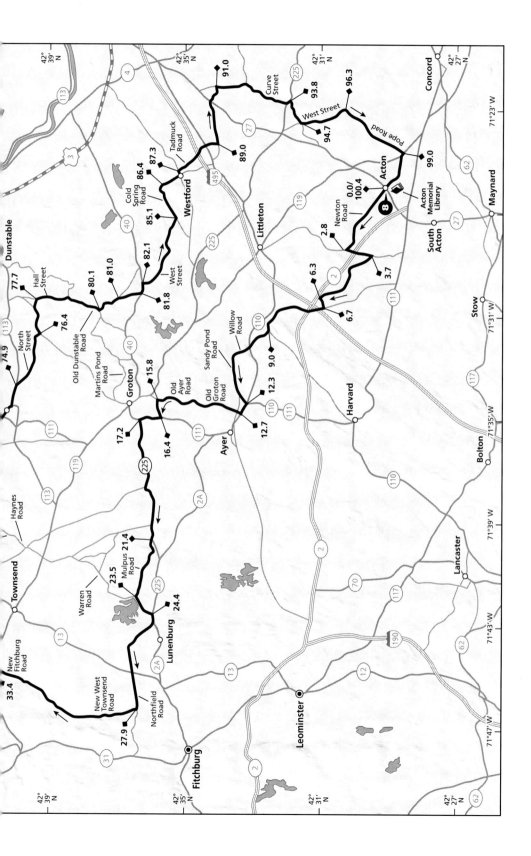

Just after a golf course, you'll turn onto New West Townsend Road, a great 5-mile stretch of country road that is extremely enjoyable on a bicycle. Be sure to stop at the Townsend Variety store at mile 33.3 along State Route 119 at the end of New West Townsend Road for food and drink before continuing the route. Three major climbs still lie ahead, and you won't have a chance to stop again until you've completed them all.

From West Townsend you'll ascend along the first long climb of the route into southern New Hampshire to enjoy more farmlands and hills as the route follows the winding path of the Souhegan River. Three more challenging climbs await. You'll find them all as you weave across Greenville, Milford, and back south through Brookline. Make note that Old Milford Road is your last major climb of the route, and also that it offers a fun, fast, and safe descent along smooth pavement as a reward after you successfully crest the top. Also, the Village Store awaits you at the bottom of the hill with food and drink.

The remainder of the route winds along the great cycling roads in Pepperell and Dunstable, Westford and Carlisle, many of which have been featured on other routes in this guide. They are all the more enjoyable after climbing the hills of New Hampshire, and they will lead you back to Acton.

Miles and Directions

0.0 Depart Acton Memorial Library, 486 Main Street, Acton, on SR 27 (Main Street).

0.1 Turn right onto Newton Road.

2.5 Road name changes to Fort Pond Hill Road.

2.8 Turn left onto Newton Road.

3.1 Road name changes to Central Street.

3.7 Turn right onto Littlefield Road.

4.7 Road name changes to Depot Road.

5.1 Bear left onto Davidson Road.

5.6 Road name changes to Bulkeley Road.

6.3 Turn left onto Foster Street.

6.7 Turn right onto Taylor Street.

8.3 Road name changes to Harvard Road.

9.0 Bear right onto Bruce Street. Caution: Rough pavement.

10.0 Road name changes to Willow Road.

10.6 Road name changes to Sandy Pond Road.

12.3 At roundabout, take the first exit onto State Route 111 (State Route 2A).

12.7 Turn right onto Groton Harvard Road.

13.7 Road name changes to Old Groton Road.

14.4 Road name changes to Old Ayer Road.

15.8 Turn left onto Peabody Street.

16.4 Turn right onto SR 111 (Farmers Row).

17.2 Turn left onto SR 225 (Long Hill Road).

18.2 Bear left onto SR 225 (West Main Street).

19.6 Bear left onto SR 225 (West Groton Road).

19.8 Bear right onto SR 225 (Groton Road).

21.4 Bear right onto Mulpus Road.

23.5 Bear left onto Townsend Harbor Road.

24.4 Turn right onto SR 2A (Massachusetts Avenue).

24.6 Keep right onto Northfield Road.

24.7 Keep right to stay on Northfield Road. Caution: Steep descent with limited visibility at end of road.

27.9 Turn right onto New West Townsend Road.

30.5 Road name changes to New Fitchburg Road.

33.4 Turn right onto SR 119 (Main Street).

33.5 Turn left onto Mason Road.

33.7 Turn right onto Dudley Road.

34.6 Turn left onto Barker Hill Road.

36.4 Enter New Hampshire. Road name changes to Townsend Road.

38.7 Road name changes to Brookline Road.

40.2 Bear left onto Old County Road.

40.9 Turn left onto Starch Mill Road.

41.8 Turn left onto Russell Road.

42.6 Turn left onto Wilton Road.

44.0 Turn right onto Greenville Road.

46.2 Bear left onto Adams Hill Road.

47.0 Turn right onto New Hampshire State Route 31 (Fitchburg Road).

49.5 Bear right onto NH 31 (Greenville Road).

51.9 Bear right onto Isaac Frye Highway.

52.1 Turn right onto Captain Clark Road.

53.5 Turn left onto Potter Road.

54.2 Turn right onto Abbot Hill Road.

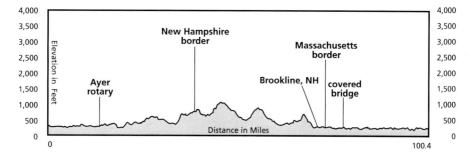

55.0 Road name changes to Mitchell Hill Road. Caution: Steep downhill to a stop sign at the end. Turn left onto Abbott Hill Road.

55.1 Road name changes to Mason Road.

60.1 Turn right onto Osgood Road.

60.2 Bear left onto Melendy Road (not marked).

61.7 Turn right onto Ruonala Road.

62.6 Turn right onto New Hampshire State Route 13.

63.2 Turn left onto Old Milford Road.

66.7 Road name changes to Steam Mill Hill Road.

66.8 Village Store, Brookline, New Hampshire.

66.9 Turn left onto New Hampshire Route 130 (Main Street).

67.4 Keep straight onto NH 130 (Pepperell Road).

68.5 Keep straight onto Pepperell Road.

69.0 Road name changes to West Hollis Road.

70.1 Enter Massachusetts. Road name changes to Brookline Street.

73.1 Turn right onto SR 111 (Hollis Street), then immediately turn left onto Groton Street.

73.7 Keep straight onto State Route 113 (Groton Street).

73.8 Bear right onto Groton Street, then immediately turn left onto Leighton Street. Caution: Pavement is very rough under the covered bridge.

74.3 Bear right onto SR 113 (Lowell Road), then immediately bear right onto Jersey Street.

74.9 Keep straight onto Jersey Street (North Street).

75.9 Road name changes to Kemp Street.

76.4 Turn left onto Groton Street.

77.4 Turn right onto School Street.

77.7 Keep right onto Hall Street.

78.4 Road name changes to Old Dunstable Road.

78.9 Turn right to stay on Old Dunstable Road.

79.3 Keep straight to stay on Old Dunstable Road.

80.1 Turn left onto Hoyts Wharf Road.

81.0 Turn right onto Flavell Road.

81.8 Turn left onto State Route 40 (Lowell Road).

82.1 Turn right onto Graniteville Road.

82.3 Road name changes to West Street.

83.6 Turn left onto North Main Street.

84.2 Turn right onto Broadway Street.

84.6 Turn right onto River Street. Road name changes 50 yards later to Graniteville Road.

85.1 Bear left onto Cold Spring Road.

86.1 Bear left onto Depot Road.

86.2 Keep right onto Lowell Road.

86.4 Turn right onto Providence Road.

87.1	Turn left onto Main Street.
87.3	Turn right onto Tadmuck Road.
89.0	Turn left onto South Chelmsford Road.
89.5	Road name changes to Parkerville Road.
90.2	Bear right onto Maple Road.
90.4	Road name changes to Common Street.
90.5	Bear right onto Proctor Road.
91.0	Bear right onto Park Road.
91.7	Road name changes to Martin Street.
92.1	Turn right onto Curve Street.
93.7	Bear left onto SR 225 (Westford Street).
93.8	Turn right onto Acton Street.
94.7	Bear left onto West Street.
96.3	Bear right onto Pope Road.
98.9	Turn right onto SR 119 (SR 2A).
99.0	Turn left onto Concord Road.
99.9	Bear right onto Nagog Hill Road.
100.3	Turn left onto SR 27 (Main Street).
100.4	Arrive back at Acton Memorial Library.

Ride Information

Local Information

Central Massachusetts Tourist Council,
30 Worcester Center Boulevard, Worcester;
www.worcester.org.

Restaurants

Acton Jazz Cafe, 452 Great Road, Acton;
(978) 263-6161; www.actonjazzcafe.com.
Dinner only.
Brookline Village Store, 12 Main Street,
Brookline, N.H.; (603) 673-8100.

Accommodations

Concord's Colonial Inn, 48 Monument
Square, Concord; (800) 370-9200, (978)
369-9200.

Holiday Inn Boxborough, 242 Adams Place,
Boxborough; (978) 263-0518.

Map

DeLorme Massachusetts Atlas & Gazetteer,
pages 26-27, 28, 38-39, 40.

9 North Andover Ramble

The North Andover Ramble explores some of the most enjoyable cycling roads north of Boston. The rural feel of these classic New England towns will inspire your pedaling, and the graceful, unspoiled town centers will invite you to relax and enjoy the ride. This tour of North Andover and Boxford is very enjoyable, with many rolling hills but no significant climbs. It's all about having fun and enjoying the ride on the North Andover Ramble.

Start: Salem Street, Andover.
Length: 33.3 miles.
Ride time: 2 hours.
Terrain: Delightfully rolling, with lots of little ups and downs. There's one hill on the ride.
Traffic and hazards: Use caution during the short segments on State Route 114. It is a very busy road. Care should also be taken during the short segment on State Route 113, which can be busy at rush hour.

Getting there: If you're heading north on Interstate 93, exit north onto State Route 125 for 2.3 miles, and then exit north onto State Route 28. Go about 3 miles and Salem Street is on the right at the traffic light adjacent to Phillips Academy. There's a tall brick tower at the intersection.

The North Andover Ramble is a bicyclist's paradise. It's a low-traffic and well-paved route along country lanes, gentleman farms, and lakesides. You'll travel through a couple of graceful, unspoiled New England town centers with stately old homes and picket fences.

The ride starts next to Phillips Academy, the classic New England preparatory school. Its large, impressive campus equals that of any college for elegance. You'll quickly cross the town line into North Andover to enjoy a beautiful mixture of estates, woods, and large, well-landscaped newer homes on good-size wooded lots. The old center of town is a gem, with a stately old church and a green framed by gracious colonial-style homes. The centerpiece of the town is Lake Cochichewick, a large, refreshingly unspoiled lake surrounded by estates and wooded hills. You'll parallel the shore and then bike past the Brooks School, another preparatory school with a magnificent campus of graceful white wooden buildings and broad fields sweeping down to the lakefront.

You'll also loop through Boxford, which is even nicer for cycling than North Andover. Boxford epitomizes the gracious suburb that is rural rather than suburban. Silk-smooth roads curve past woodlots and horse farms with pastures crisscrossed by rustic white wooden fences, rambling old homes, and impressive new homes harmoniously integrated with the landscape on two- and three-acre forested lots. The center of town is another New England classic, with a fine old church, a country

Riders on the quiet back roads of Boxford

store, and stately old homes. After looping through Boxford you'll pick up the route of the short ride back in North Andover in time to bike along the estate-lined southern shore of Lake Cochichewick.

Miles and Directions

0.0 Proceed down Salem Street, away from SR 28.

0.1 Turn left onto Highland Road.

1.3 Road name changes to Hillside Road.

1.5 Bear left onto SR 125 (Andover Bypass).

1.7 Keep right onto local road(s).

1.8 Turn right onto SR 114 (Salem Turnpike). Caution: SR 114 is very busy.

2.0 Turn left onto Hillside Road.

2.5 Bear left onto Chestnut Street.

3.1 Bear right onto Andover Street.

3.4 Keep straight onto Andover Street (Great Pond Road).

3.5 Road name changes to Great Pond Road.

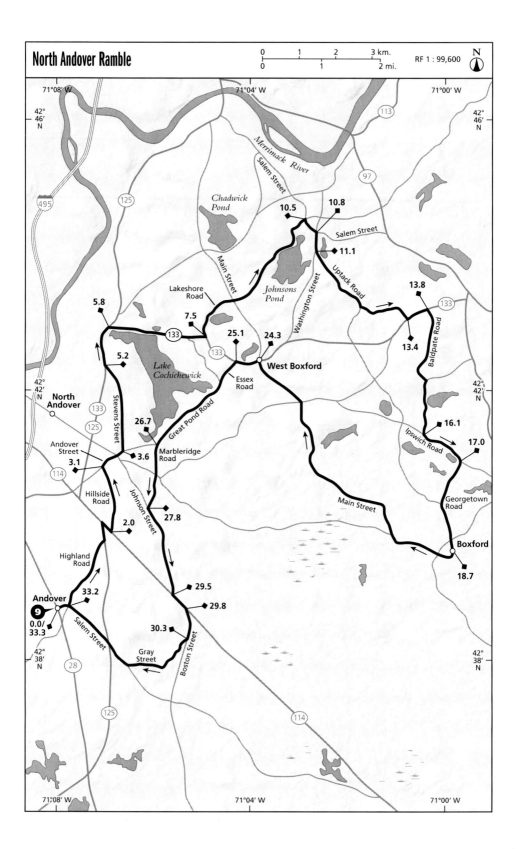

North Andover Ramble

0   1   2   3 km.
0   1   2 mi.

RF 1 : 99,600   N

3.6 Turn left onto Stevens Street.

4.6 Keep straight onto Osgood Street.

5.2 Bear right onto SR 125 (State Route 133).

5.8 Bear right onto SR 133 (Great Pond Road).

7.5 Turn left onto Lakeshore Road.

9.5 Road name changes to Center Street.

10.5 Turn right onto Salem Street.

10.8 Turn right onto Washington Street.

11.1 Bear left onto Uptack Road.

12.2 Road name changes to West Street.

13.4 Turn left onto SR 133 (Andover Street).

13.8 Turn right onto Baldpate Road.

15.2 Turn right to stay on Baldpate Road.

16.1 Bear left onto Ipswich Road.

17.0 Bear right onto Georgetown Road.

18.4 Road name changes to Elm Street.

18.7 Bear right onto Main Street.

24.3 Turn left onto SR 133 (Washington Street).

24.7 Turn left onto Essex Street.

25.1 Bear left onto Great Pond Road.

26.7 Bear left onto Marbleridge Road.

27.8 Bear left onto Johnson Street.

29.5 Bear left onto SR 114 (Salem Turnpike). Caution: SR 114 is a very busy road.

29.8 Keep right onto Boston Street.

30.3 Bear right onto Gray Street.

31.0 Road name changes to Gray Road.

31.6 Keep straight onto Salem Street.

32.1 Turn right onto SR 125 (By Pass Road).

32.2 Keep left onto Salem Street.

33.3 Arrive back at Salem Street starting point.

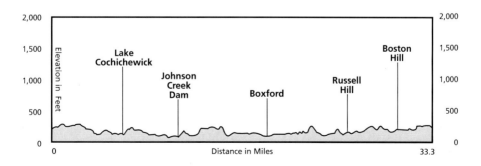

Ride Information

Local Information
North of Boston Convention & Visitors Bureau, 17 Peabody Square, Peabody; (800) 443-3332, (978) 977-7760 ; www.northof bosoton.org.

Restaurants
Arthur's Corner Pizzeria, 1060 Osgood Street, North Andover; (978) 685-1500.

Accommodations
Andover Inn, 4 Chapel Avenue, Andover; (800) 242-5903, (978) 475-5903.

Map
DeLorme Massachusetts Atlas & Gazetteer, page 29.

10 Newbury Ramble

The Newbury Ramble takes you exploring among the broad salt marshes, prosperous farmland, and gracious estates just inland from the coast south of Newburyport. You'll pass imposing mansions built by sea captains and merchants in Newburyport and also The Governor's Academy, the oldest boarding school in the country. The area abounds with country roads that promise relaxed and delightful biking.

Start: Rupert A. Nock Middle School, on Low Street in Newburyport.
Length: 22 miles.
Ride time: 1.5 hours.
Terrain: Gently rolling, with one hill.

Traffic and hazards: Most of the roads are quiet, but traffic along State Route 1A can be busy in downtown Newbury. State Route 133 can be busy at times and has narrow shoulders.

Getting there: If you're heading north on Interstate 95, take the Scotland Road exit (exit 56). Turn right onto Scotland Road for 3 miles to end (Low Street), and left for 0.2 mile to school on right. If you're heading south, exit east from I-95 onto State Route 113 (take exit 57). Go 0.3 mile to Low Street (not marked) on right, at traffic light. Turn right onto Low Street and go 1.3 miles to school on left, just past the traffic light.

Situated at the mouth of the Merrimack River, Newburyport became a thriving shipbuilding community during the 1700s and then evolved into a commercial center. The most successful sea captains and merchants built elegant mansions along a 2-mile stretch of High Street, which you'll go along at the beginning of the ride.

The downtown and waterfront areas, lying just off the route between High Street and the river, have been restored and are worth exploring. Gracious brick buildings from the Federal era line State Street, the main downtown street. At the base of State Street, next to the river, is Market Square, where the old brick mercantile buildings

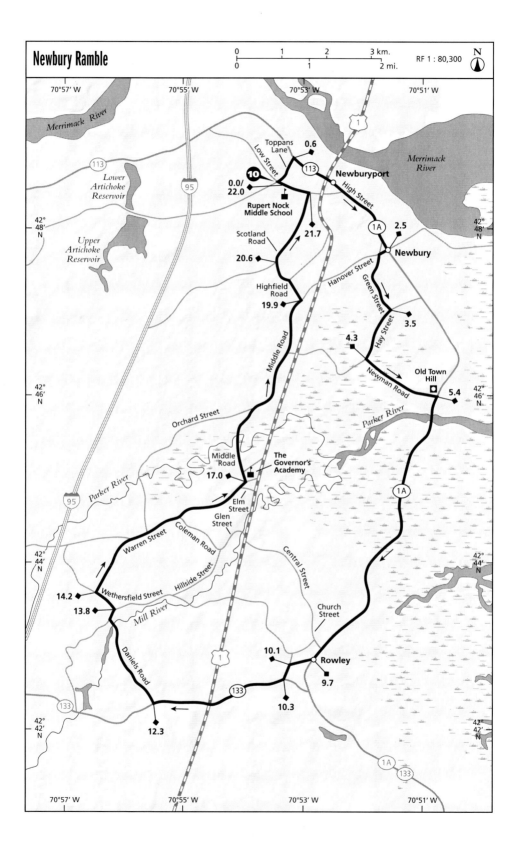

Newbury Ramble

0   1   2   3 km.
0   1   2 mi.

RF 1 : 80,300

N

Merrimack River

70°57' W   70°55' W   70°53' W   70°51' W

113

Lower Artichoke Reservoir

95

Toppans Lane

Low Street

0.6

113

Newburyport

High Street

Merrimack River

0.0/ 22.0

10

Rupert Nock Middle School

21.7

1A

2.5

42° 48' N

Upper Artichoke Reservoir

42° 48' N

Scotland Road

20.6

Newbury

Hanover Street

Green Street

Highfield Road

19.9

Hay Street

3.5

4.3

Newman Road

Old Town Hill

5.4

42° 46' N

Middle Road

42° 46' N

Orchard Street

Parker River

Parker River

95

Middle Road

17.0

The Governor's Academy

1A

Elm Street

Glen Street

Warren Street

Coleman Road

42° 44' N

Central Street

42° 44' N

14.2

Wethersfield Street

Hillside Street

13.8

Mill River

Daniels Road

Church Street

10.1

9.7

Rowley

42° 42' N

1

10.3

133

12.3

42° 42' N

1A

133

70°57' W   70°55' W   70°53' W   70°51' W

have been recycled into a mini-mall of antiques shops, galleries, and craft shops. The result is tasteful rather than touristy. The library, built in 1771, is an especially fine building, as is the stately granite Custom House, built in 1835 and now a maritime museum. Adjoining the downtown are narrow streets lined with old wooden homes.

Just south of Newburyport is Newbury, a small town consisting mainly of salt marshes and farmland. In the village center are several historic homes from the 1600s and 1700s. Just outside town you'll pass Old Town Hill, a small glacial drumlin rising 170 feet above the Parker River. Maintained by the Trustees of Reservations, it offers an outstanding view of the Parker River, Plum Island, and the broad estuary separating it from the mainland.

From Newbury you'll head along SR 1A past broad salt marshes and well-kept farms to Rowley, an attractive small town with several antiques shops and even an antiques flea market. As numbered routes go, SR 1A is one of the best in the state for bicycling—smooth, flat, not heavily traveled, and with a good shoulder. In Rowley you'll head inland, and after a few miles you'll go through the gracious campus of the The Governor's Academy, founded in 1763. The return to Newburyport leads along country lanes as you follow the Parker River a short distance, cross it, and proceed past stately old farmhouses and immaculate fields.

Miles and Directions

0.0   Depart Rupert Nock Middle School, 70 Low Street, Newburyport.

0.2   Turn right onto Toppans Lane.

0.6   Turn right onto SR 113 (High Street).

1.2   Road name changes to SR 1A (High Street).

2.5   Turn right onto Hanover Street.

2.6   Bear left onto Green Street.

3.5   Turn right onto Hay Street.

4.3   Turn left onto Newman Road.

5.4   Turn right onto SR 1A (High Road).

9.7   Keep left onto Summer Street.

10.1   Turn left onto Bradford Street.

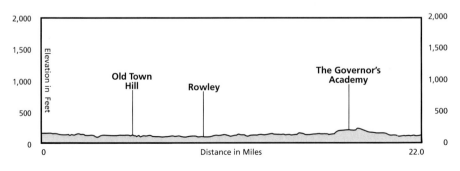

10.3	Keep straight onto SR 133 (Haverhill Street).
12.3	Turn right onto Daniels Road.
13.0	Keep straight onto Dodge Road.
13.7	Turn right onto Long Hill Road.
13.8	Bear left onto Wethersfield Street.
14.2	Bear right onto Warren Street.
15.2	Road name changes to Elm Street.
17.0	Turn left onto Old Road. Road name changes to Middle Road.
19.9	Turn left onto Highfield Road.
20.6	Turn right onto Scotland Road.
20.7	Road name changes to Parker Street.
21.2	Keep straight onto Graf Road.
21.7	Turn left onto Low Street.
22.0	Arrive back at Rupert Nock Middle School.

Ride Information

Local Information

North of Boston Convention & Visitors Bureau, 17 Peabody Square, Peabody; (800) 443-3332, (978) 977-7760; www.northof bosoton.org.

Restaurants

The Grog, 13 Middle Street, Newburyport; (978) 465-8008. Off route.

Accommodations

Morrill Place, 209 High Street, Newburyport; (978) 462-2808, (978) 462-9966.

Map

DeLorme Massachusetts Atlas & Gazetteer, page 19.

11 Ipswich River Ramble

Ipswich ranks as one of the most beautiful towns in the state, both architecturally and geographically. Beyond the center of town is an unspoiled mixture of wooded hills; broad, gently rolling horse farms and gracious country estates; vast salt marshes stretching to the horizon; the Great Neck peninsula rising steeply from the bay; and magnificent 4-mile-long Crane Beach, New England's finest beach north of Cape Cod. The Ipswich River Ramble is an enjoyable flat route with a few short hills along the route.

Start: Municipal parking lot behind the business block at State Route 1A and Topsfield Road in downtown Ipswich. Entrance is on Hammatt Street, which is off SR 1A, 1 block north of Topsfield Road. Some parking spots are restricted. You can also park on Hammatt Street.
Length: 20.4 miles.

Ride time: 1.5 hours.
Terrain: Flat, with a tough hill to get to the Crane estate on Castle Hill and a couple of short hills on Great Neck.
Traffic and hazards: The short section on SR 1A in the center of Ipswich can be busy and congested.

Getting there: Take SR 1A North to Ipswich Road. Follow it for 5.5 miles to the center of Ipswich. Take a left onto Depot Square, and bear right at the intersection onto Hammatt Street.

The ride starts from the center of Ipswich, lying between two greens and surrounded by a marvelous variety of buildings, all painstakingly restored and maintained, that span every architectural style from early colonial days to 1900. If you're a historic-house enthusiast, you'll exult: The town has more pre-Revolutionary homes—some going back to the 1600s—than any other locale north of Williamsburg, Virginia.

You'll head first to Crane Beach through an idyllic landscape of salt marshes, horse paddocks, and estates. The majestic Crane mansion, resembling a palace from the Italian Renaissance, crowns Castle Hill near the beach. The wide beach is unique in that it is almost completely unspoiled—no hot dog stands, no cottages, no anything except sand, dunes, and lots of people on a hot day. The beach and the Castle Hill estate are owned by the Trustees of Reservations.

From Crane Beach you'll return to the center of town and then head through an endless expanse of salt marshes to the Great Neck peninsula, just north of Crane Beach. Rising steeply from the bay as a succession of four round drumlins, the peninsula is bordered by salt marshes on the west, the broad Plum Island Sound on the north, the southern tip of Plum Island on the east, and Crane Beach on the south. The roads rimming the peninsula offer spectacular views of this unique seascape. From Great Neck you return through the salt marshes to Ipswich.

Christian Wainwright House, circa 1741

Miles and Directions

0.0   Take a right out of parking lot onto Hammatt Street, heading toward Main Street.

0.1   Turn right onto State Route 133 (SR 1A).

0.5   Turn left onto Argilla Road.

1.0   Turn right onto Heartbreak Road.

1.7   Turn left onto SR 133 (Essex Road).

2.8   Turn left onto Northgate Road.

3.6   Bear right onto Argilla Road.

3.8   Goodale Orchards Winery.

5.9   Keep straight onto local road(s).

6.1   Enter the Crane Beach parking lot, loop around, and head back out.

6.4   Bear right onto Argilla Road.

6.6   Turn right onto Castle Hill access road.

6.8   Bear right and follow road to loop around Castle Hill.

7.6   Bear right onto access road to return to Argilla Road.

7.8   Turn right onto Argilla Road.

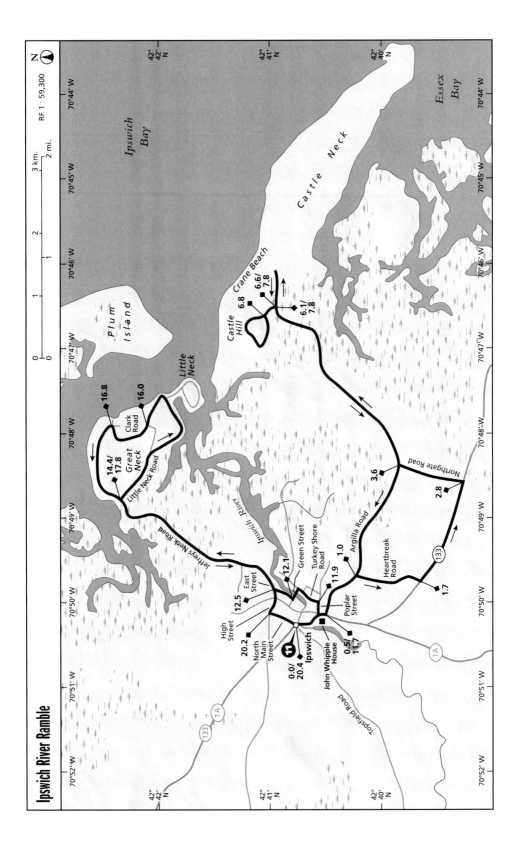

Ipswich River Ramble

RF 1 : 59,300

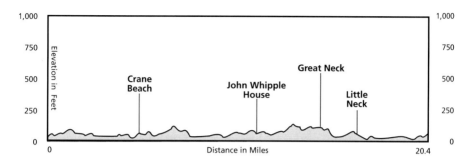

11.7	Turn right onto SR 133 (SR 1A).
11.8	Turn right onto Poplar Street.
11.9	Turn left onto Turkey Shore Road.
12.1	Turn left onto Green Street, then immediately turn right onto Water Street.
12.5	Bear right onto East Street.
12.7	Road name changes to Jeffreys Neck Road.
14.4	Keep right onto Little Neck Road.
15.8	Road name changes to Bayview Road.
16.0	Bear right onto Clark Road.
16.8	Turn left onto Colby Road. Road name changes to North Ridge Road after 100 yards.
17.8	Road name changes to Jeffreys Neck Road.
19.5	Road name changes to East Street.
19.9	Turn right to stay on East Street.
20.0	Road name changes to High Street.
20.2	Turn left onto Manning Street.
20.4	Turn left onto SR 133 (SR 1A), then immediately turn right onto Hammatt Street and arrive back at parking lot.

Ride Information

Local Information

North of Boston Convention & Visitors Bureau, 17 Peabody Square, Peabody; (800) 443-3332, (978) 977-7760 ; www.northof bosoton.org.

Local Events and Attractions

Goodale Orchards Winery/Russell Orchards, 143 Argilla Road, Ipswich; (978) 356-5366.

Restaurants

Choate Bridge Restaurant, 3 South Main Street, Ipswich; (978) 356-2931.

Ithaki Mediterranean Cuisine, 25 Hammatt Street, Ipswich; (978) 356-0099.

Accommodations

The Inn At Castle Hill, 280 Argilla Road, Ipswich; (978) 412-2555.

Town Hill Bed & Breakfast, 16 North Main Street, Ipswich; (978) 356-8000, (800) 457-7799; www.townhill.com.

Map

DeLorme Massachusetts Atlas & Gazetteer, page 30.

12 North Shore Cruise

A flat tour of some great North Shore suburbs, this ride will take you through the centers of Topsfield, Ipswich, Georgetown, and Boxford. Each town is worth visiting in its own right; touring them together makes for an even more enjoyable journey. You'll follow the Ipswich River to the sea before heading through the back country roads of Rowley on your way to Georgetown and the heavily wooded winding roads of Boxford. This is a great route for the tourist, with frequent stops available for refreshments and many historic sites to ponder. This is also a great route for more serious training on fast, flat roads.

Start: Village Shopping Center, Main Street, Topsfield.
Length: 44.4 miles.
Ride time: 2.5 to 3 hours.
Terrain: Mostly flat with only one short climb coming out of Georgetown.

Traffic and hazards: Ipswich Road can be busy at rush hour. Care should be taken on the short segments on State Routes 133 and 97, which can be busy at times and have small shoulders.

Getting there: From Interstate 95 North, take exit 50/U.S. Route 1–Topsfield. Go 3.0 miles and take a left onto SR 97 North. Go 0.5 mile and take a left at the stop sign onto Main Street. Go 0.2 mile and take a right into Village Shopping Center.

Which is more fun, riding along the coast enjoying expansive ocean views or riding on winding heavily wooded back country roads? Well, on the North Shore Cruise, you'll get both! The route can be approached in different ways for a variety of cycling experiences. As a tour, you'll pass through four quaint New England town centers where you can score refreshments, hang out on expansive common areas, and see historic buildings and monuments. If you're looking for a good workout, this route has many long stretches along flat roads where you can really put in a measured effort. All told, this is one of my personal favorites, combining many of my favorite roads near my home in the North Shore.

Topsfield is home to America's oldest agricultural fair, the Topsfield Fair, established in 1818. The show has been held annually since its inception, except for three years during the Civil War and three years during World War II. True to its roots, the fair continues "to promote and improve the agricultural interests of farmers and others in Essex County" with an extensive array of related events. It also has added a large amusement game and ride contingent in order to attract and entertain children, and the fair has proven to be a popular event year after year.

Topsfield also has a large town common area surrounded by wonderful old trees and a variety of historic buildings. You'll pass right through this area at the beginning of the ride before heading out to Ipswich, a seacoast town with a rich

An expansive green in the center of Topsfield

history of its own. Colonized as Agawam in 1633, Ipswich covers 33 square miles of forests, farmlands, dunes, and marshes. One of its great attractions is the former estate of the Crane family, which encompassed what are now Castle Hill, Crane Beach, and Crane Wildlife Refuge. Many outdoor concerts and other popular town events take place at the site of the fifty-nine-room mansion known as The Great House that sits on top of Castle Hill with a view of Crane Beach and the Crane Wildlife Refuge.

Winding away from the beach, you'll make your way through the quiet back roads of Rowley before emerging in Georgetown and exploring its back roads and downtown area. This would be a good place to plan a stop if you haven't made one already. You will pass through Boxford center, but there are really no food or services available there. Boxford is by far the most rural of the towns along the route. What you will find in Boxford, however, are great winding cycling roads. You'll need to pay attention to some of their quirks. For instance, you'll actually feel like you're changing roads at a few intersections when you're simply trying to follow the Main Street stretch.

North Shore Cruise

RF 1 : 121,500

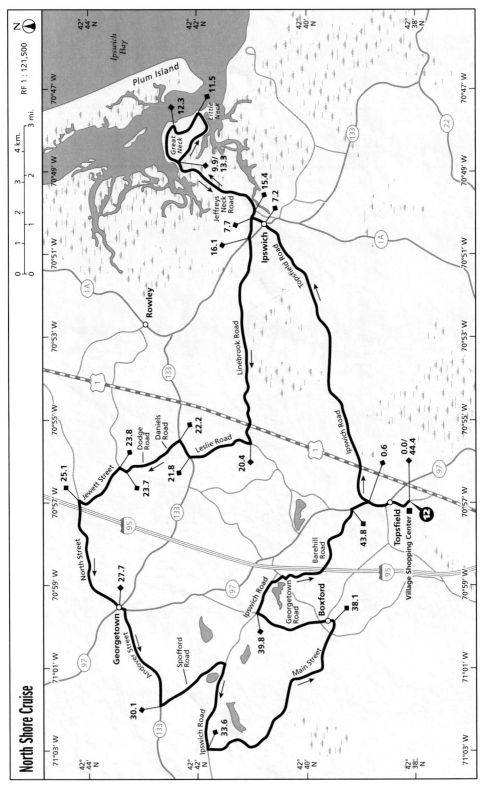

Miles and Directions

0.0 Go left out of the Village Shopping Center on Main Street (north).

0.2 Bear right (north) onto SR 97 (Main Street).

0.6 Bear right onto Ipswich Road.

3.3 Road name changes to Topsfield Road.

7.0 Road name changes to Market Street.

7.2 Go straight at stop sign onto North Main Street, up a short hill and bear left at the fork in the road to stay on North Main Street (passing behind the church).

7.6 Turn right (east) onto East Street.

7.7 Turn left at stop sign, remaining on East Street.

8.2 Road name changes to Jeffreys Neck Road as you follow a sharp left-hand bend in the road.

9.9 Keep right onto Little Neck Road.

11.4 Road name changes to Bayview Road.

11.5 Bear right (north) onto Clark Road.

12.3 Turn left (north) onto Colby Road.

12.4 Road name changes to North Ridge Road (Northridge Road).

13.3 Road name changes to Jeffreys Neck Road.

15.0 Road name changes to East Street.

15.4 Turn right to stay on East Street.

15.6 Road name changes to High Street.

16.0 Bear left (west) onto Short Street.

16.1 Take a sharp left at lights and an immediate right onto Linebrook Road (immediately after Dunkin' Donuts). Caution: Very busy intersection.

20.4 Bear right (northwest) onto Leslie Road.

21.8 Turn right (northeast) onto Haverhill Street (SR 133).

22.2 Turn left (northwest) onto Daniels Road (big sign for Rowley Country Club).

23.0 Bear left onto Dodge Road (not marked). *Stay straight turns into Dodge*

23.7 Bear right (northeast) onto Long Hill Road.

23.8 Turn left at stop sign (northwest) onto Wethersfield Street.

24.0 Road name changes to Jewett Street.

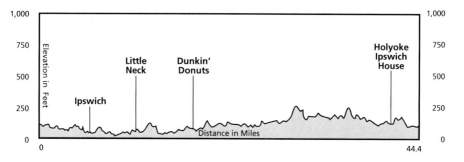

25.1	Turn left to stay on Jewett Street.
26.1	Bear left (west) onto North Street (not marked).
27.7	Bear right (southwest) onto SR 133 (SR 97).
30.1	Turn left (southeast) onto Spofford Road (not to be confused with the left just before it called Spofford Street).
31.7	Turn right (west) onto Ipswich Road.
33.6	Turn left (south) onto Main Street. Caution: After the short uphill section, the road comes down quickly into a split and you must bear left to stay on Main Street, crossing a lane of oncoming traffic.
38.1	Go straight at stop sign onto Elm Street (not marked). Historic Holyoke Ipswich House is on the corner on your right.
38.4	Road name changes to Georgetown Road.
39.8	Turn right at fork (east) onto Ipswich Road.
40.6	Bear right (south) onto Pond Street (not marked).
40.8	Turn right at stop sign (south) onto Depot Road (not marked), then immediately turn left (south) onto Bare Hill Road (not marked).
43.4	Turn right (south) onto SR 97 (Haverhill Road).
43.8	Bear right (south) onto SR 97 (Main Street).
44.2	Bear left (south) onto Main Street.
44.4	Arrive back at Village Shopping Center.

Ride Information

Local Information

Ipswich Visitor Information Center, Hall Haskell House, 36 South Main Street, (State Route 1A) Ipswich; (978) 356-8540.

Local Events and Attractions

Topsfield Fair, 207 Boston Street, SR 1; (978) 887-5000; www.topsfieldfair.org.

Restaurants

Topsfield House of Pizza, 32 Main Street, Topsfield; (978) 887-9642.

Accomodations

Miles River Country Inn—a Bed & Breakfast Inn, 823 Bay Road, Hamilton; (978) 468-1210; www.milesriver.com.

Town Hill Bed & Breakfast, 16 North Main Street, Ipswich; (800) 457-7799, (978) 356-8000; www.townhill.com.

Map

DeLorme Massachusetts Atlas & Gazetteer, pages 29, 30.

13 Topsfield Ramble

The Topsfield Ramble is a tour exploring three elegant old North Shore communities connected by delightful secondary roads winding past horse farms, country estates, and ponds and along the Ipswich River. Topsfield is best known for its two giant annual fairs, the American Crafts Exposition in July and the Topsfield Fair in October. The latter is one of the country's oldest agricultural fairs, running since 1818. Surrounding the town are gentleman farms and estates spreading up rolling hills and the marshes of the Ipswich River, along which is the state's largest Audubon sanctuary.

Start: Village Shopping Center, Main Street, Topsfield
Length: 23.7 miles.
Ride time: 1.5 to 2 hours.
Terrain: Flat.

Traffic and hazards: Most of the route is along low-traffic roads, but they can get busy at rush hour. Care must be taken when navigating both downtown Ipswich and Topsfield.

Getting there: Take Interstate 95 to the Topsfield Road exit (exit 52). Turn right onto Topsfield Road and travel 1.4 miles (1.6 if you're coming from the north) to High Street Extension, which bears right just before a white church. Bear right and just ahead turn right at the crossroads and stop sign. The shopping center is just ahead on your right.

You start from Topsfield, a handsome town with one of the finest traditional New England centers in the state. The large green is framed by an exceptionally fine classic white church and a marvelous Victorian town hall built in 1873. Adjoining the green is the Parson Capen House, built in 1681 and open to visitors.

From Topsfield you'll head through gently rolling farmland to Ipswich, a jewel of a town both geographically and architecturally. It boasts more pre-Revolutionary houses, some from the 1600s, than any other place in America north of Colonial Williamsburg. With the continuing efforts of a preservation-conscious citizenry, these buildings have been painstakingly restored and maintained. The center of town lies between a north green and a south green and contains a wonderful mixture of buildings of every architectural style from the early colonial period to the turn of the century. Many of these houses are open to visitors; if you're a historic-house enthusiast, you can spend the entire day in town. If you want to see just one house, the one to visit is the John Whipple House, built in 1640. It has an herb garden and period furnishings.

The Ipswich River courses through town and passes under the graceful stone-arched Choate Bridge, built in 1764 and one of the oldest original bridges in the country. You'll parallel the Ipswich River and wind through carefully maintained horse farms and estates to Wenham, another gracious town with a stately white church and old town hall. Shortly before Wenham you'll pass Asbury Grove, a Methodist campground containing small Gothic-style cottages and a central taber-

Topsfield Ramble

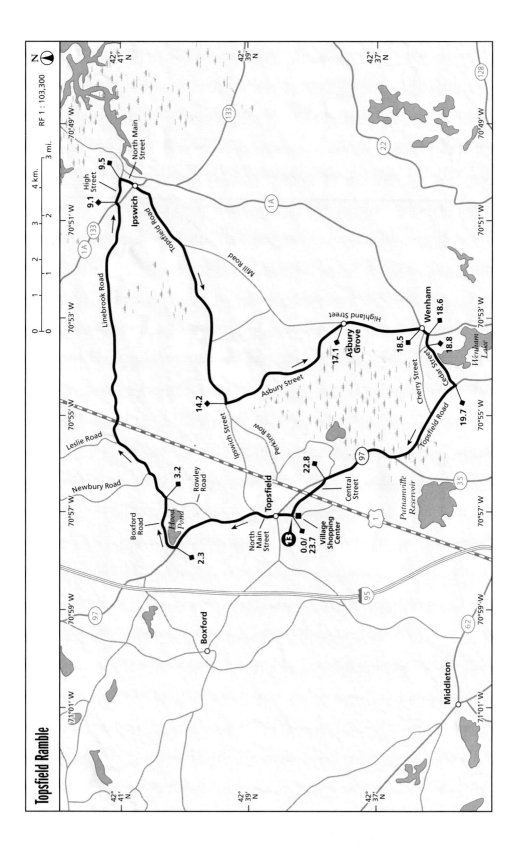

RF 1 : 103,300

Choate Bridge Pub, Ipswich

nacle. It is similar to Oak Bluffs in Martha's Vineyard but not as extensive or orna-
mented. Asbury Grove was founded in 1858.

Next to the Wenham town hall is the Claflin-Richards House, built in 1664. It
adjoins the Wenham Historical Association and Museum, which maintains a fascinating display of dolls, toys, and games from the 1800s. It's open in the afternoon
every day except Saturday. From Wenham it's a short ride back to Topsfield, passing
Wenham Lake and rolling, open hillsides.

Miles and Directions

0.0 Turn left out of parking lot onto State Route 97, heading north.

0.2 Bear right onto SR 97 (Main Street).

0.6 Bear left onto SR 97 (Haverhill Road).

2.3 Turn right onto Pond Street.

2.4 Turn right onto Boxford Road.

3.2 Bear left onto Linebrook Road.

3.8 Turn right to stay on Linebrook Road.

9.0 Road name changes to Short Street.

9.1 Bear right onto High Street.

9.5 Turn right onto North Main Street.

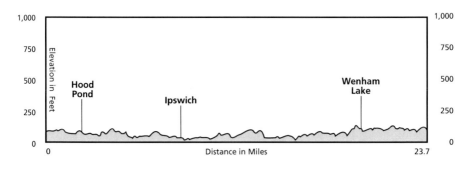

9.7 Road name changes to Market Street when you cross State Routes 1A/133 in center of Ipswich.

9.9 Road name changes to Topsfield Road.

13.6 Road name changes to Ipswich Street.

14.2 Turn left onto Asbury Street.

17.1 Bear right onto Highland Street.

17.9 Road name changes to Arbor Street.

18.5 Turn right onto SR 1A (Main Street). Caution: Busy road.

18.6 Turn right onto Cherry Street.

18.8 Turn left onto Cedar Street.

19.7 Turn right onto SR 97 (Topsfield Road).

21.5 Keep left onto Wenham Road.

21.7 Bear right onto High Street.

22.2 Bear left onto SR 97 (High Street).

22.8 Bear left onto Central Street.

23.7 Turn right onto Main Street and arrive back at Village Shopping Center.

Ride Information

Local Information

North of Boston Convention & Visitors Bureau, 17 Peabody Square, Peabody; (800) 443-3332, (978) 977-7760 ; www.northof bosoton.org.

Local Events and Attractions

Topsfield Fair, 207 Boston Street, Route 1; (978) 887-5000; www.topsfieldfair.org.

Restaurants

Choate Bridge Restaurant, 3 South Main Street, Ipswich; (978) 356-2931.

Accommodations

Miles River Country Inn—a Bed & Breakfast Inn, 823 Bay Road, Hamilton; (978) 468-1210; www.milesriver.com.

Town Hill Bed & Breakfast, 16 North Main Street, Ipswich; (800) 457-7799, (978) 356-8000; www.townhill.com.

Map

DeLorme Massachusetts Atlas & Gazetteer, pages 29, 30.

14 Harold Parker Cruise

Harold Parker State Forest, 20 miles north of Boston, is just more than 3,000 acres of central hardwood-hemlock-white pine forest. A popular site for a variety of recreational opportunities such as hiking, mountain biking, fishing, hunting, horseback riding, swimming, camping, and picnicking, the state forest makes for a great start to this relaxing bike route. The Harold Parker Cruise will take you through the quiet, wooded, winding roads of Boxford, Georgetown, Topsfield, and Middleton.

Start: Harold Parker State Forest parking lot at trailhead.
Length: 42.4 miles.
Ride time: 2.5 to 3 hours.
Terrain: Rolling hills and winding back roads, with a few steep uphill sections.

Traffic and hazards: Mostly quiet back roads. Care must be taken crossing State Route 114, a very busy road, and along State Route 97 in Topsfield.

Getting there: From Interstate 95 North, take exit 41 onto State Route 125 and travel for 2.6 miles. Turn right onto Gould Road and then immediately left onto Harold Parker Road. Drive to the end and directly across the street is the trail parking lot.

Departing from the Harold Parker State Forest, you'll head north through the peaceful, winding back roads of Boxford on your way to Georgetown center. Georgetown, though incorporated in 1838, was actually settled some 200 years earlier. In 1638 a small group of families from Rowley, England, sailed across the ocean to settle in the area now known as Georgetown. By the spring of the following year, more than 200 individuals called the area home, and they helped one another build humble dwellings in preparation for the coming winter. The town would come to flourish as its variety of industries grew, including clothing, cigar, soap, and furniture manufacturers. Today Georgetown is a quiet bedroom community with a bustling town center.

From Georgetown, the Harold Parker Cruise loops back through Topsfield, a quaint New England town with an expansive town common and classic white church and town hall buildings. As in Georgetown, Topsfield has a variety of shops and restaraunts for lunch or a quick snack. Next you'll weave through the rural roads of Boxford on your way to Middleton, a commuter town of 5,000 residents, before heading into Lynnfield. Weaving through Lynnfield and back up through North Reading is very enjoyable riding. The roads are winding and some small hills provide a bit of a challenge. Finally, you'll loop through the state forest and pass the placid Field Pond, where you're likely to see people fishing in the warmer months or playing ice hockey in the winter months.

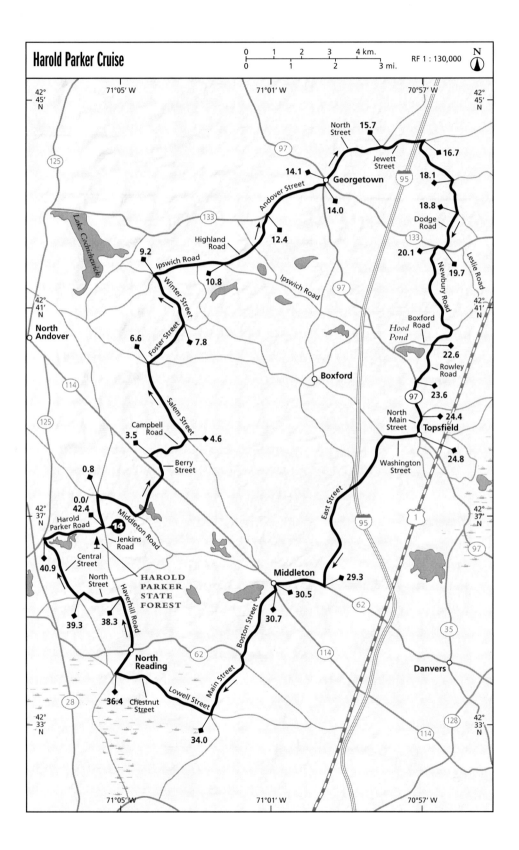

Miles and Directions

0.0 Take a right out of parking lot onto Jenkins Road (not marked).

0.8 Turn right onto Salem Street.

1.0 Road name changes to Middleton Street.

1.8 Turn left onto Harold Parker Road.

2.9 Road name changes to Berry Street as it crosses SR 114.

3.5 Turn right onto Ash Street.

3.7 Road name changes to Campbell Road.

4.6 Bear left onto Salem Street.

6.6 Turn right onto Foster Street.

7.8 Turn left onto Winter Street.

9.2 Turn right onto Dale Street.

9.4 Road name changes to Ipswich Road.

10.8 Bear left onto Highland Road.

11.6 Road name changes to Spofford Street as it crosses Spofford Road.

12.4 Turn right onto State Route 133 (Andover Street).

14.0 Turn left onto SR 133 (SR 97).

14.1 Bear left onto North Street.

15.7 Bear right onto Jewett Street.

16.7 Turn right to stay on Jewett Street.

17.8 Road name changes to Wethersfield Street.

18.0 Bear right onto Long Hill Road.

18.1 Turn left onto Dodge Road.

18.8 Turn right to stay on Dodge Road.

19.2 Keep straight to stay on Dodge Road.

19.7 Bear right onto SR 133 (Haverhill Street).

19.8 Bear left onto Boxford Road.

20.1 Turn left onto Newbury Road.

22.0 Keep straight onto Linebrook Road.

22.6 Turn left to stay on Linebrook Road.

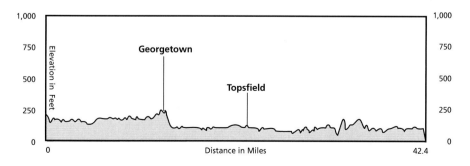

23.0 Road name changes to Rowley Road.

23.6 Bear left onto SR 97 (Haverhill Road).

24.4 Bear right onto SR 97 (Main Street).

24.8 Bear right onto Washington Street.

26.5 Road name changes to Endicott Road.

27.3 Road name changes to East Street.

29.3 Turn right onto State Route 62 (Maple Street).

30.5 Turn left onto SR 114 (SR 62).

30.7 Turn right onto SR 62 (Boston Street).

33.0 Road name changes to Main Street.

34.0 Turn right onto Lowell Street.

35.3 Road name changes to Chestnut Street.

36.4 Turn right onto Haverhill Street.

38.3 Turn left onto North Street.

39.3 Bear right onto Central Street.

40.2 Road name changes to Gould Road.

40.9 Turn right onto Harold Parker Road.

42.4 Arrive back at start.

Ride Information

Local Information

North of Boston Convention & Visitors Bureau, 17 Peabody Square, Peabody; (800) 443-3332, (978) 977-7760; www.northof bosoton.org.

Accommodations

Sheraton Colonial Hotel & Golf, 1 Audubon Road, Wakefield; (781) 245-9300.

Map

DeLorme Massachusetts Atlas & Gazetteer, page 29.

15 Lynnfield Ramble

An easy and relaxing ride through two small bedroom towns north of Boston, the Lynnfield Ramble is flat and fun. You'll pass through two modest town centers and visit a variety of residential outposts, including the winding roads around Pillings Pond. The North Reading town center offers a great resting spot on top of a large grass-covered hill that is home to its grand old meetinghouse, built in 1829.

Start: Lynnfield Plaza, at the intersection of Salem and Summer Streets in Lynnfield.
Length: 22.9 miles.
Ride time: 1.5 to 2 hours.
Terrain: Mostly flat.

Traffic and hazards: Mostly residential areas with a few back roads. You will need to take care at a few busy intersections, but most roads have light to moderate traffic with good shoulders.

Getting there: From State Route 128 North, take exit 43 (Walnut Street). At the end of the ramp, turn right and immediately left at the lights. Follow for 0.8 mile to shopping center on your left.

The Lynnfield Ramble covers some great residential areas just north of SR 128 that make for very enjoyable cycling. The route circumnavigates Pillings Pond, which sprawls across 86 acres of southern Lynnfield. The pond is a great scenic spot even though it's densely populated with year-round homes on three sides.

The ride quickly arrives in Lynnfield town center, a quaint spot with town buildings and retail businesses surrounding a triangular town green. Across from the green is the old burying ground, where a variety of headstones can be found peeking out from the many trees that have grown in since 1728.

On your way to North Reading, you will cover several miles of smooth, flat roads, including many with a surprisingly rural feel considering your proximity to SR 128. North Reading town center will offer an almost irresistible stop at the steep, grassy hill that holds the old meetinghouse and classic white bandstand. Ryer's Store is conveniently located just across the street from the green should you need a drink or a quick snack.

The ramble ends with a tour of the north side of Pillings Pond on narrow and winding roads typically traveled only by those who live on the pond.

Miles and Directions

0.0 Start at Lynnfield Plaza shopping center. Turn right out of the parking lot onto Salem Street.

0.8 Turn right at lights onto Walnut Street. Caution: busy intersection followed by highway on/off ramps on Walnut Street.

1.5 Turn right onto Thomas Road, up a short hill.

Lynnfield Ramble

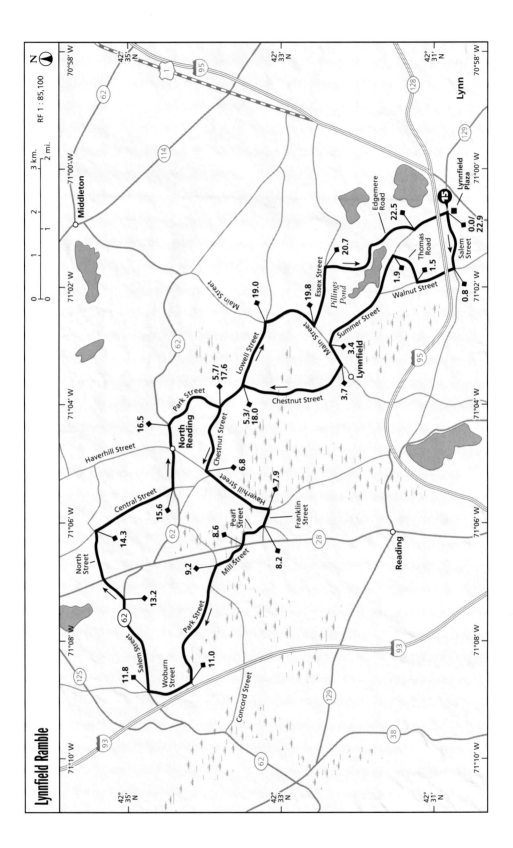

1.9 Turn left at stop sign onto Summer Street (not marked).

3.3 Bear left at fork in road as you approach Lynnfield town center.

3.4 Turn left at stop sign onto Main Street.

3.7 Turn right onto Chestnut Street.

5.3 Turn left at stop sign, remaining on Chestnut Street. (not marked).

5.7 Turn left to stay on Chestnut Street.

6.8 Turn left at stop sign onto Haverhill Street.

7.9 Turn right onto Franklin Street. (not marked).

8.2 Turn right onto Pearl Street (marked on opposite side of street only).

8.6 Go straight through stop sign to Mill Street. Caution: Use care crossing State Route 28; it is a very busy road, and the visibility is limited at this intersection.

9.2 Turn left at stop sign at end of road onto Park Street (not marked).

11.0 Turn right onto Woburn Street (not marked), just before the bridge.

11.8 Turn right at lights onto Salem Street (State Route 62).

12.7 Cross town line into North Reading.

13.2 Turn left onto North Street.

14.3 Turn right onto Central Street. Caution: This turn is at the bottom of a short, very steep hill with a flashing yellow light at the intersection.

15.6 Turn left at stop sign onto SR 62 and proceed into North Reading town center.

16.5 Turn right onto Park Street, just after crossing the bridge.

17.6 Turn left at stop sign onto Chestnut Street.

18.0 Bear left onto Lowell Street.

19.0 Turn right at stop sign onto Main Street.

19.8 Turn left onto Essex Street.

20.7 Turn right onto Pillings Pond Road.

21.2 Turn left onto Oak Ridge Terrace. Caution: The road is very narrow and rough in spots, but traffic is light as it is typically traveled only by people who live on the lakefront.

21.6 Turn right onto Edgemere Road (not marked), which follows the perimeter of the pond.

21.9 Turn right at stop sign, remaining on Edgemere Road.

22.4 Turn right at stop sign onto Archer Road.

22.5 Turn left at stop sign onto Summer Street.

22.9 Turn right and arrive back at parking lot for Lynnfield Plaza.

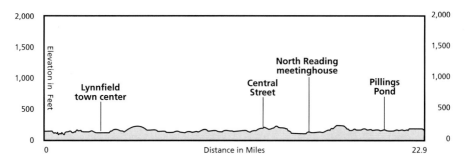

Ride Information

Local Information

Lynn Area Chamber of Commerce, 100 Oxford Street, Lynn; (781) 592-2900.

North of Boston Convention & Visitors Bureau, 17 Peabody Square, Peabody; (800) 443-3332, (978) 977-7760; www.northof bosoton.org.

Restaurants

Lynnfield House of Pizza, Lynnfield Plaza, 18 Post Office Square, Lynnfield; (781) 593-0818.

99 Restaurant, 317 Salem Street, Lynnfield; (781) 599-8119. A pub-style chain.

Accommodations

Sheraton Colonial Hotel, One Audubon Road, Wakefield; (781) 245-9300.

Restrooms

0.0 Various restaurants in plaza at ride start.

Map

DeLorme Massachusetts Atlas & Gazetteer, page 29.

16 Marblehead Ramble

Explore the wonderfully classic coastal New England town of Marblehead, cruising along a beautiful coastline peppered with many parks and places of historic interest. Marblehead Neck offers a visit to Chandler Hovey Park, a beautiful spot with a nearly 360-degree view of the sea and a 105-foot-tall cast-iron lighthouse built in 1896. From the Neck, you'll travel to downtown Marblehead, where you'll be much better off on a bike than in a car as you weave along the narrow streets that are lined with beautifully restored historic homes. The pace is easy and the route contains many opportunities to stop for food, shopping, or visiting many historic sites.

Start: From the Lynn shoreline near the Nahant causeway

Length: 19.2 miles.

Ride time: 1.5 to 2 hours.

Terrain: A mostly flat, scenic coastline ride with great water views that wanders through some of the dense, historical streets of the town of Marblehead.

Traffic and hazards: Traffic can be heavy on some short segments of the route on hot summer days that attract lots of people to the beach. Care must be taken during a couple miles of the route that pass through very narrow, twisting streets of downtown Marblehead.

Getting there: From the south, head north on State Route 1A into Lynn. When SR 1A turns left, continue straight on the main road for 0.5 mile to the rotary. Go three quarters of the way around the rotary. Park as soon as it's legal or on the service road on the left (inland) side of road.

From the north, head south on U.S. Route 1 to State Route 60. Go east on SR 60 for 2 miles to SR 1A, at the second rotary. Continue with directions from the south, heading north on SR 1A into Lynn.

Chandler Hovey Park, with a view of Marblehead Harbor

If you enjoy spectacular ocean views and classic New England towns, this ride is for you. You will be able to explore the beautiful park areas along the coast, see many historic homes, and enjoy a plethora of shops and restaurants. One popular spot that you'll pass by both near the start and finish of the ride is Popo's Old Fashioned Hot Dogs, where you can sample their world-famous steamed or grilled hot dogs with your choice of a wide variety of toppings—a great source of energy for your ride or a tasty reward near the end (takeout only).

You may also find it inspiring to know that you're riding through the hometown of one of America's most successful professional cyclists, Tyler Hamilton. Riding these same roads, Tyler began a career that would lead him to help Lance Armstrong on three Tour de France victories before setting out on his own to win an Olympic gold medal in cycling, among other accomplishments. Tyler's old cycling club still organizes a very successful and very popular race around Marblehead Neck each spring, a short course that provides a wonderful opportunity to see professional cyclists in action.

When you're ready to ride, the Marblehead Ramble heads up the Lynn shoreline, crosses the town line into Swampscott after the first mile, and proceeds on into Marblehead just a bit farther along the route. After a brief tour through some cozy neighborhoods, sneaking ocean peaks between historic homes, you'll head across a

Marblehead Ramble

RF 1 : 65,520

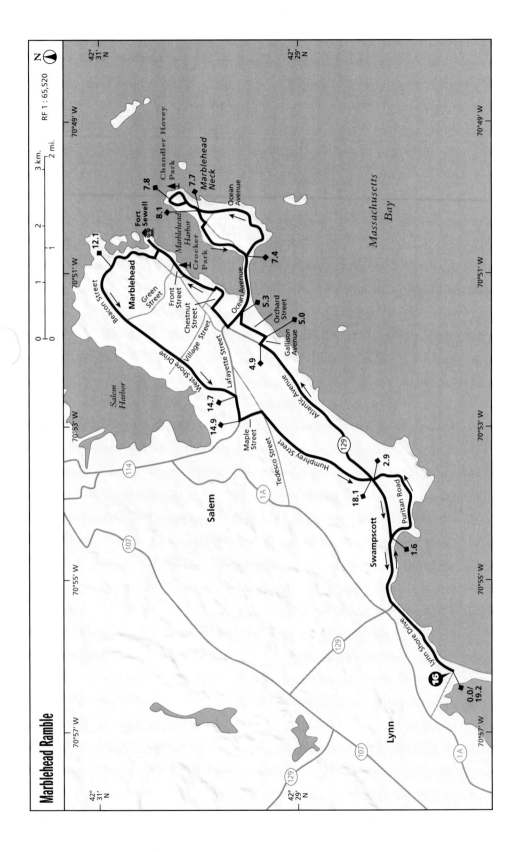

dramatic causeway crossing onto Marblehead Neck. The causeway offers stunning ocean views, along with a unique view of the Boston skyline on a clear day. Your tour of Marblehead Neck will weave through some of the most stunning homes with the most picturesque views in Marblehead. On the farthest point out on the Neck, be sure to stop at Chandler Hovey Park for a look at the historic lighthouse, to take a well-deserved rest on one of the many benches, and to get a great view of Marblehead Harbor, one of the yachting and sailing capitals of New England.

After you come off the Neck, you'll head downtown through the maze of narrow streets lined with restored antique homes—there are more than 200 homes in Marblehead that were built prior to the Revolutionary War. Here you'll explore routes much easier traveled by bicycle than by car. Though it can get a bit congested, particularly during hot summer days, the downtown area offers many shops and spots to eat lunch or grab an ice-cream treat. Take your time to soak it all in. Also be sure to stop and explore Crocker Park and Fort Sewell as you pass through the downtown area. Fort Sewell, isolated on its own small peninsula, contains the remains of a Revolutionary fort. Just north of town is Old Burial Hill, one of the state's outstanding historic cemeteries, with many slate headstones dating from the 1700s and earlier stretching up the terraced hillside.

On the ride back toward the start, you'll have ample opportunity to spin freely for a few miles to work off that ice-cream stop or to work up an appetite for that Popo's hot dog just over the line in Swampscott. You'll go back along Lynn Shore Drive to the start. Be careful negotiating the rotary. It may be best to stop prior to the rotary and cross Lynn Shore Drive by foot to get back to your car. The rotary traffic can be quite heavy at times.

Miles and Directions

0.0 Start at Lynn Shore Drive near rotary (Don John Aliferis Memorial Circle) across from Christies Restaurant by playground. Head north on Lynn Shore Drive, following the ocean on your right.

1.0 Cross town line into Swampscott and travel past shops and restaurants.

1.6 Bear right at stoplights onto Puritan Road. Stay on main road (Puritan Road), where you will see ocean views that include a view of the Boston skyline.

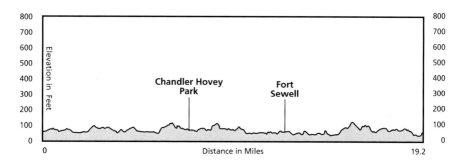

2.9 Turn right at stop sign onto Atlantic Avenue.

3.9 Cross town line into Marblehead.

4.9 Turn right onto Gallison Avenue. Street name is marked, but watch your mileage for this turn or you could miss it.

5.0 Turn left onto Orchard Street.

5.3 Turn right onto Beach Street.

5.5 Turn right at stop sign, remaining on Beach Street.

6.1 Turn right onto Ocean Avenue at end of causeway, where you will get another view of the Boston skyline.

7.4 Bear right at intersection to remain on Ocean Avenue.

7.7 Turn left onto Follet Street.

7.8 Arrive Chandler Hovey Park, where you can view the lighthouse and panoramic views of Marblehead, rest on one of the many benches, and use the public restrooms. When leaving Chandler Hovey Park, turn right (left if you choose not to stop at the park) and follow road to stop sign. Turn right.

8.1 Bear right at fork in road onto Harborview Road (not marked).

8.3 At bottom of hill, turn right onto Ballast Lane (marked on opposite side of the road) toward the ocean.

8.8 Turn right at stop sign onto Harbor Avenue (not marked) to cross back across the causeway.

9.8 Turn right at stoplights onto Atlantic Avenue. Take care on this more heavily trafficked road as you head toward downtown Marblehead.

10.1 Turn right onto Chestnut Street, where you will see several retail shops.

10.3 At end of Chestnut Street, turn left onto Cliff Street.

10.4 At end of Cliff Street, turn left onto Commercial Street (not marked) and make a quick right onto Gregory Street (street sign hidden by tree).

11.0 Turn right at stop sign onto Union Street. Stay right past Boston Yacht Club.

11.1 Go straight at stop sign. Take care as you enter a tight, twisty area of Marblehead where sidewalks disappear and the road narrows. It is a tight squeeze for cars, bikes, and pedestrians. You will pass by a bunch of shops and a good lunch spot, The Landing.

11.6 Turn right onto unmarked road.

11.7 Turn right onto Orne Street.

12.0 Bear left to remain on Orne Street.

12.1 Turn right at stop sign onto Beacon Street, which becomes West Shore Drive.

14.7 Turn right at stoplights onto Lafayette Street.

14.9 Turn left at stoplights onto Maple Street.

15.2 Bear right at light onto Humphrey Street (do not take sharp right onto Tedesco Street).

16.7 Bear right at yield sign, remaining on Humphrey Street.

17.9 Keep left on Humphrey Street.

18.1 Turn left onto Lynn Shore Drive. Proceed south, with the ocean on your left.

19.2 Arrive back at start.

Ride Information

Local Information

Marblehead Chamber of Commerce, 62 Pleasant Street, Marblehead; (781) 631-2868; www.visitmarblehead.com.

North of Boston Convention & Visitors Bureau, 17 Peabody Square, Peabody; (800) 443-3332, (978) 977-7760; www.northof bosoton.org.

Local Events and Attractions

Michael Schott Memorial Circuit Race, Marblehead; www.ccbracing.com.

Restaurants

Christie's Restaurant, 17 Lynnway, Lynn; (781) 598-1122.

Popo's Hot Dogs, 168 Humphrey Street, Swampscott; (781) 592-9992.

The Landing Restaurant, 81 Front Street at State Street, Marblehead Harbor; (781) 639-1266; www.thelandingrestaurant.com.

Accommodations

The Marblehead Inn, 264 Pleasant Street, Marblehead; (781) 639-9999; www.marble headinn.com.

Restrooms

7.8 Chandler Hovey Park.

Map

DeLorme Massachusetts Atlas & Gazetteer, pages 30, 41, 42.

17 Minuteman Ramble

This is a tour of four classic New England communities northwest of Boston, and you'll pass several historic sites related to the battles of Lexington and Concord, the first skirmishes of the Revolutionary War. Between the town centers lies a gently rolling landscape of gentleman farms, some estates surrounded by acres of open land, and gracious colonial-style homes and farmhouses.

Start: Minute Man National Historical Park in Lexington.
Length: 23.8 miles.
Ride time: 1.5 to 2 hours.
Terrain: Gently rolling, with one tough hill.

Traffic and hazards: The numbered routes and even some of the back roads along this route are very busy during weekday commute times. It is best to ride this route on a weekend or at midday during the week.

Getting there: Take State Route 128 to exit 30B and make the second right onto Old Massachusetts Avenue. A dirt parking lot is on the right.

At the beginning of the ride, you'll skirt Hanscom Field, a former Air Force base; then, in a flash, you'll enter a delightful landscape of horse farms, rolling meadows, and old clapboard homes. If you wish you can ride on the Battle Road Trail, a dirt bicycle and pedestrian path that attempts to follow the original roadway as it existed in 1775.

From here it's a couple of miles into Concord, a town unique as both a historic and literary center. Nearly a century after the American Revolution, Concord was

Minuteman Ramble

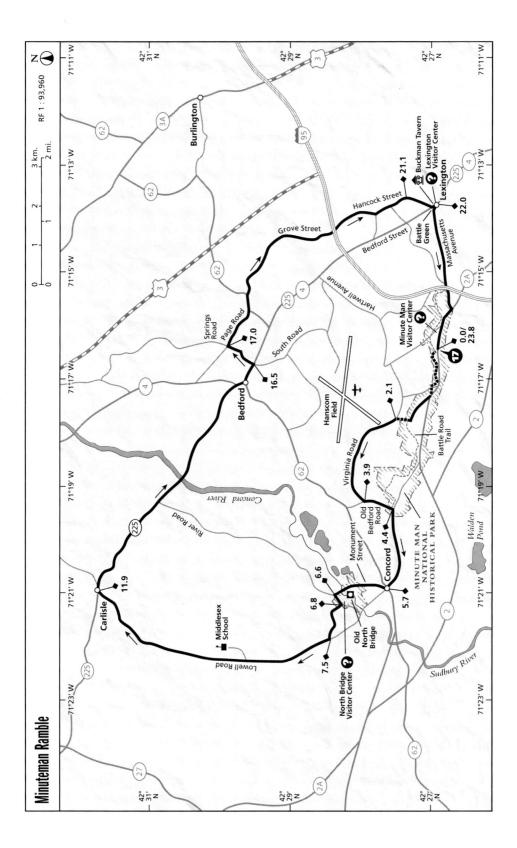

RF 1 : 93,960

N

3 km.   2 mi.

Burlington

42° 31' N
42° 29' N
42° 27' N

71°11' W
71°13' W
71°15' W
71°17' W
71°19' W
71°21' W
71°23' W

Buckman Tavern
Lexington Visitor Center
Lexington   21.1
22.0

Hancock Street

Bedford Street
Battle Green
Massachusetts Avenue

Grove Street

Minute Man Visitor Center
0.0/ 23.8

Hartwell Avenue

Battle Road Trail

Page Road
Springs Road
17.0
16.5
Bedford
South Road

Hanscom Field

2.1

Virginia Road

3.9

MINUTE MAN NATIONAL HISTORICAL PARK

Concord River

Old Bedford Road

Concord   4.4

Walden Pond

River Road
225
11.9
Carlisle

Monument Street
6.6
6.8

Middlesex School

Old North Bridge

5.7

Lowell Road
7.5

North Bridge Visitor Center

Sudbury River

Old North Bridge, Concord

the home at one time or another of Hawthorne, Emerson, Thoreau, and the Alcotts. They are all buried in Sleepy Hollow Cemetery, just outside town. Coming into Concord, you'll pass the Wayside, where the Alcotts and Hawthorne once lived; the Orchard House, another Alcott home; and the Emerson House. Just north of town, a half mile off the route, is Concord's most famous landmark, the Old North Bridge. It's a lovely spot despite the daily onslaught of hundreds of sightseers and school-children on field trips—a simple, gently bowed wooden bridge over the lazy Concord River, replaced several times since the Revolution. Adjacent to the bridge is the Old Manse, built in 1770 by Emerson's grandfather and the residence of both Hawthorne and Emerson, and the North Bridge Visitor Center, housed in an elegant brick mansion.

The ride then heads north from Concord past the Old North Bridge and the visitor center to the elegant, unspoiled rural town of Carlisle. You'll go along a ridge with fine views across broad, open meadows, and then past the gracious campus of the Middlesex School, an exclusive preparatory school with broad lawns and handsome redbrick buildings. The center of town is a jewel, with a stately white church standing over the green, an old wooden schoolhouse on top of the hill, a fine brick Victorian library, and a delightful country store.

From Carlisle it's not far to Bedford, a pleasant residential community with an unusually large and elegant white church in the center of town. The section from Bedford to Lexington passes through gracious residential areas, going past an appealing mixture of tastefully designed newer homes and fine older ones set off by shade trees and broad lawns. Finally you arrive at famed Lexington Green, also called Battle Green, scene of the first American casualties of the Revolution. The large, triangular, tree-shaded green, with a stately white church at its head, is a delightful place to rest. At one corner of the green is a fine old statue in honor of the minutemen, built in 1799. Across the street from the green is the Buckman Tavern, where the minutemen assembled to await the British, a superbly restored and maintained old tavern with its original furnishings intact.

Miles and Directions

0.0 Depart Old Massachusetts Avenue, Lexington.

0.1 Bear right onto State Route 2A (Massachusetts Avenue).

0.4 Keep straight onto SR 2A (North Great Road).

1.1 Turn right onto Hanscom Drive.

1.8 Turn left onto Old Bedford Road (do not go into airport).

2.1 Road name changes to Virginia Road at corner.

3.9 Turn left onto Old Bedford Road.

4.4 Keep straight onto SR 2A (Lexington Road).

5.7 Merge onto SR 2A (State Route 62) at rotary.

5.8 Bear right onto SR 62 (Monument Street—second right in rotary).

6.6 Turn left onto Liberty Street.

6.8 Turn right onto Estabrook Road.

7.1 Keep straight onto Barnes Hill Road.

7.5 Turn right onto Lowell Road.

9.7 Road name changes to Concord Street.

11.9 Turn right onto State Route 225 (Westford Street), take the first exit out of rotary onto Bedford Road (SR 225).

16.5 Turn left onto Springs Road.

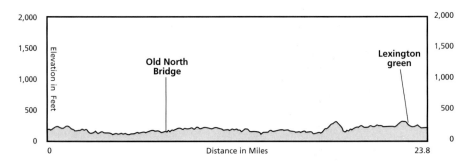

17.0	Turn right onto Page Road.
17.7	Keep straight onto SR 62 (Page Road).
17.9	Keep right onto Page Road.
18.8	Road name changes to Grove Street.
20.4	Turn right onto Burlington Street.
20.8	Burlington Road merges into Blake Road. Follow for 100 yards into rotary. Take the first right out of rotary onto Hamilton Road.
21.1	Road name changes to Coolidge Avenue as it crosses Revere Street. Follow for 50 yards and turn right onto Hancock Street.
21.8	Bear right onto Harrington Road.
22.0	Bear right onto Massachusetts Avenue.
23.5	Turn right onto SR 2A (Marrett Road).
23.7	Turn right onto Old Massachusetts Avenue.
23.8	Arrive back at start.

Ride Information

Local Information

Greater Boston Convention & Visitors Bureau, 2 Copley Place, Suite 105, Boston; (888) SEE-BOSTON, (617) 536-4100; www.bostonusa.com.

Lexington Visitor Center, 1875 Massachusetts Avenue, Lexington; (781) 862-2480.

Restaurants

Buckman Tavern, 1 Bedford Street, Lexington; (781) 862-1703.

Accommodations

Battle Green Motor Inn, 1720 Massachusetts Avenue, Lexington; (781) 862-6100.

Concord's Colonial Inn, 48 Monument Square, Concord; (800) 370-9200, (978) 369-9200.

Restrooms

6.2 Rest rooms at Old North Bridge in Concord.

Map

DeLorme Massachusetts Atlas & Gazetteer, page 40.

18 Bolton Berlin Challenge

Interstate 495 is often viewed as the demarcation point separating greater metropolitan Boston from Massachusetts' vast rural areas. Nowhere is this more apparent than on the Bolton Berlin Challenge. The convenience of the highly developed starting area in South Acton is quickly contrasted by long, open stretches of country roads where fast food—or any type of modern convenience—disappears. Many of the roads go mile after mile without even passing a house. Load up on supplies before heading out on this one, there's only one real stop for food and restrooms along the way. That inconvenience is easily outweighed by the beauty of the expansive views you'll enjoy at the top of the route's climbs and the winding descents that are each climb's reward. Your camera won't capture many historic sites on this route; this is a ride for bonding with nature rather than sightseeing.

Start: South Acton Commuter Rail Station.
Length: 59.4 miles.
Ride time: 3.5 to 4.5 hours.
Terrain: Hilly at times with a few sharp climbs. Each climb comes with a reward that includes a spectacular view and a great descent.
Traffic and hazards: Most roads are very lightly traveled by cars. There are just a couple of crossings of busy roads along the way.

Getting there: From State Route 2 West, take exit 43 (State Route 111) toward South Acton. Turn left onto State Route 27 and go 1 mile to Central Street. Take a sharp right (hairpin turn) onto Central Street and a quick left into the commuter lot. The parking meters are not active on weekends.

Head out of the commuter lot, ride a short stint on busy SR 27, then turn right and head for some serious country roads. This ride will take you from civilization to roads where you'll have to create some excitement of your own. This is a great route for conversation paced rides where you won't be disturbed by passing cars very frequently, for enjoying a solo outing to gather your thoughts, or for serious training to challenge yourself with a quick pace on the climbs and skillful bike handling on the descents.

Within a few miles you'll be on the back roads of Stow, passing by the Minuteman Airfield, a small municipal airport. You'll ride on relatively flat terrain until about mile 12 and the route's ascent up the aptly named Long Hill Road. At the end of Long Hill Road, you'll have a brief brush with civilization again along moderately busy State Routes 117 and 85 on a short transition to Century Mill Road, which leads you into Bolton.

Bolton was incorporated in 1738 and is primarily a residential and agricultural community. It is the home of Bolton Orchards, a thriving fifth-generation farm with 250 acres producing fruits and vegetables. From Bolton, the route goes south to Berlin, an even more rural community that registered only 2,380 residents in the 2000 census.

Riders on Central Street

On route to Berlin, Sawyerhill Road offers miles of riding surrounded by only trees and fresh air, which are punctuated at the end with an apple orchard and a horse farm. Here you'll also have a chance to grab a bite to eat at Berlin Orchards Store, where you can get coffee, ice cream, and other goodies. You'll need an energy burst for the steep ascent up the next section of Sawyerhill Road (after crossing State Route 62) that starts the next segment of the ride. While this is a tough climb with some very steep spots, your effort is rewarded with the first of the expansive views of the countryside on this ride. Soak it all in because you'll soon be flying down a long, enjoyable descent at full speed.

A good portion of the route continues to explore more of the wonderful Berlin countryside with an opportunity to stop at Bagel Makers, a cycle-friendly deli with great sandwiches, tables inside and out, and restrooms. Fill your water bottles because there isn't another opportunity to do so until you reach Harvard center, some 20 miles farther along the route.

Harvard is a wonderful old Massachusetts town with prevalent small-town traditions, such as its Apple Blossom Festival. Most town activities take place on the enormous town common, a great spot to relax and rest, and to refill your water bottles. There's a working water fountain at the southeast corner. Across the street is a general store where more supplies can be had. There's one more climbing section before this ride is through, so it's a good idea to fuel up at this point.

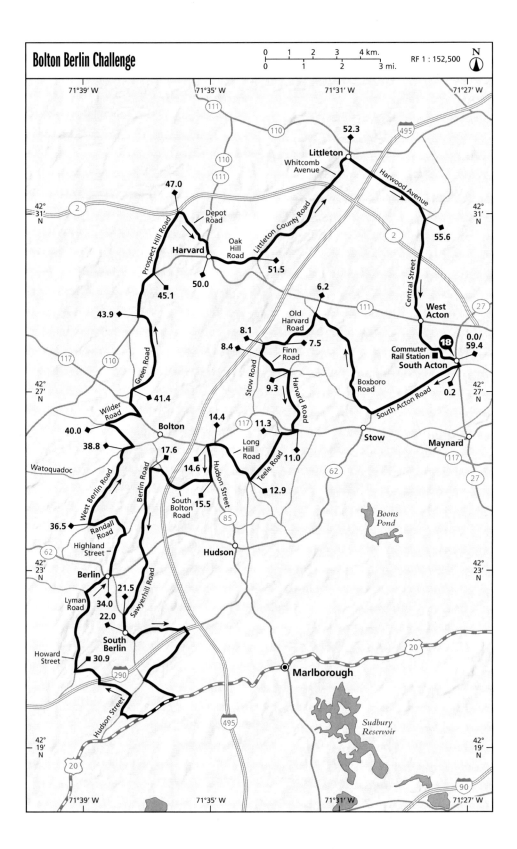

Bolton Berlin Challenge

0 1 2 3 4 km.
0 1 2 3 mi.

RF 1 : 152,500

N

Once you descend from Harvard, you begin to visit civilization again and some slightly busy roads of Littleton and Boxboro.

Miles and Directions

0.0 Turn right out of commuter lot onto Central Street.

0.1 Turn right onto SR 27.

0.2 Turn right onto Maple Street.

0.3 Bear left onto Stow Road.

0.5 Bear right to stay on Stow Road. Road name changes to South Acton Road.

2.9 Road name changes to Boxboro Road.

3.4 Bear right to remain on Boxboro Road.

5.3 Bear left onto Chester Road (not marked).

5.6 Bear left onto Burroughs Road (not marked).

6.2 Turn left onto Old Harvard Road.

7.5 Turn right onto Eldridge Road.

8.1 Turn left onto Stow Road.

8.4 Turn left onto Finn Road.

9.3 Turn right onto Harvard Road (not marked).

10.6 Turn right onto Hiley Brook Road.

10.9 Keep straight on Hiley Brook Road.

11.0 Cross SR 117 and turn right onto Old Bolton Road.

11.3 Turn left onto Maple Street. Road name changes to Teele Road.

12.9 Turn right onto Long Hill Road (not marked).

14.0 Bear left to remain on Long Hill Road.

14.4 Turn left onto SR 117.

14.6 Turn left onto SR 85.

15.5 Turn right onto Century Mill Road.

16.5 Bear right onto South Bolton Road.

17.2 Turn left onto Farm Road (not marked).

17.6 Turn left onto Berlin Road.

18.4 Bear left onto Frye Road (not marked).

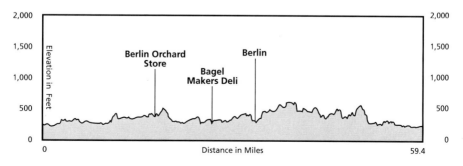

19.8 Berlin Orchards Store.

19.8 Keep straight ontp Sawyerhill Road at SR 62.

21.5 Turn left onto Pleasant Street.

22.0 Bear left onto South Street at the post office.

22.2 Turn left three-quarters of the way around the rotary.

22.4 Turn right onto River Road.

23.2 Turn right onto Bridge Road. Road name changes to Bigelow.

23.7 Turn left onto Donald D. Lynch Boulevard.

23.9 Turn right onto Bigelow Street.

24.1 Turn right at stop sign onto Robin Hill Road.

25.8 Turn left onto Boundary Street.

26.8 Turn right onto U.S. Route 20.

27.4 Bagel Makers.

27.8 Bear right onto East Main Street.

28.3 Turn right onto Allen Street.

28.5 Keep straight on Allen Street at Hudson Street.

28.6 Turn right onto Rice Road.

29.3 Bear left onto Colburn Street.

29.6 Turn left onto Bearfoot Road.

30.1 Turn right onto Whitney Street (not marked).

30.2 Turn left onto Maynard Street.

30.5 Bear left to remain on Maynard Street.

30.9 Turn right onto Howard Street.

31.5 Bear left to remain on Howard Street.

33.0 Bear left onto Lyman Road.

33.2 Turn right onto Linden Street.

33.9 Turn right onto SR 62.

34.0 Turn left onto Carter Street to the center of Berlin.

34.3 Keep straight on Carter Street. Road name becomes Highland Street.

35.2 Turn left onto Randall Road at Berlin Country Club sign.

35.7 Turn left to remain on Randall Road.

36.5 Turn sharp right onto Peach Hill Road, which becomes West Berlin Road after crossing Sawyer Road.

37.8 Cross Sawyer Road onto West Berlin Road.

38.8 Turn right onto Watoquadoc Road (not marked).

39.1 Turn right onto Old Bay.

40.0 Take a sharp hairpin turn onto Wilder Road. (not marked).

40.8 Turn left onto Sampson Road.

41.1 Keep straight on Sampson Road and cross SR 117 (use caution).

41.4 Turn right onto Green Road.

42.1	Turn left onto Bare Hill Road.
43.4	Keep straight onto West Bare Hill Road.
43.9	Turn right onto State Route 110.
45.1	Turn left onto Prospect Hill Road.
47.0	Turn right onto Depot Road.
48.1	Turn right onto SR 110.
48.5	Turn left onto Old Littleton Road at stop sign in Harvard center.
49.9	Turn right onto Oak Hill Road.
50.0	Bear left onto Oak Hill Road.
50.9	Bear left onto Oak Hill Road at Woodchuck Hill.
51.3	Turn left onto Cleaves Hill Road.
51.5	Bear left onto Littleton County Road.
51.7	Road name changes to Whitcomb Avenue.
52.0	Turn left onto Sampson Road.
52.1	Turn right onto Oak Hill.
52.3	Proceed straight across Taylor Street and over the railroad tracks, turn right onto Harwood Avenue immediately after crossing the railroad tracks.
53.5	Keep straight on Harwood Avenue at Foster Street.
54.6	Turn right onto Tahattawan Road.
55.0	Turn right onto Newtown Road.
55.6	Bear right onto Central Street.
57.8	Proceed straight across SR 111, remaining on Central Street.
58.0	Bear left, remaining on Central Street.
59.4	Return to start.

Ride Information

Local Information
Central Massachusetts Tourist Council,
30 Worcester Center Boulevard, Worcester;
www.worcester.org.

Local Events/Attractions
Apple Blossom Festival, usually held the Saturday before Mother's Day on the Harvard Common.

Restaurants
Bagel Makers, 345 West Main Street, Northborough, (508) 393-6618.
Sorrento's Brick Oven Pizzeria, 251 Main Street, Acton; (978) 264-9006.
South Acton Convenience Store, 134 Main Street, Acton; (978) 263-9889.

Accommodations
Charlotte's House Bed & Breakfast, 96 South Bolton Road, Bolton; (978) 779-5005.
Holiday Inn Boxborough, 242 Adams Place, Boxborough; (978) 263-8701.

Restrooms
0.0 Various fast food restaurants at the intersection of SR 27 and SR 111 in South Acton on route to start.
27.4 Bagel Makers Deli.

Map
DeLorme Massachusetts Atlas & Gazetteer, pages 39, 40.

19 Needham Fitness Cruise

Based on what is believed to be the longest consecutive running weekly group ride in all of Massachusetts (if not beyond), the Needham Fitness Cruise is built for cycling enjoyment. It has a convenient starting point just off a major highway (State Route 128), yet it traverses the quiet back roads of Needham, Dover, and Sherborn with many long stretches of uninterrupted riding along thickly tree-lined streets, open farmlands, and quiet residential areas.

Start: Nahanton Park, Newton (on the Needham line).
Length: 41.3 miles.
Ride time: 2.5 to 3 hours.

Terrain: Many flat sections with some small and moderate hills spread throughout the ride.
Traffic and hazards: The ride is primarily along quiet roads, but the first couple of miles can be busy during the week when businesses are open. A couple of turns require extra caution.

Getting there: Take exit 19B from SR 128. Follow Highland Avenue to the first set of lights and turn left onto Hunting Road. Turn left at the next set of lights onto Kendrick Street. Kendrick Street crosses over SR 128 and then turns into Nahanton Street as you cross the Charles River and enter Newton. Nahanton Park is on the left, immediately after crossing the river. Go slowly as it is easy to miss.

The Charles River Wheelmen Saturday Fitness Ride has run uninterrupted (year-round) each Saturday since April Fools Day of 1997 and has become a staple of cycling in the metropolitan Boston area. Neither intense summer heat nor bone-chilling cold has deterred the core riders of this classic ride. In fact, the ride has endured many rain, hail, sleet, and snow storms—along with all-out blizzards. Its 346th consecutive ride took place in the middle of the blizzard of 2003. Rest assured that if you choose to embark on the Needham Fitness Cruise route on a Saturday morning at 8:30 A.M. you won't be riding alone.

The route, originally designed by Pete Knox, accurately reflects the enthusiasm and energy of the regular riders and their penchant for paceline riding. The route has many long stretches on smooth tree-lined streets. With 1,870 feet of climbing along its 42 miles, the ride offers ample opportunity to challenge yourself or your riding partners along the way. Notably, because the regular group likes to cruise along these great roads as long as possible, there isn't a stop for food or water until mile 34. Pack appropriately.

The ascent from just above the water level of the Charles River to the heights of the SR 128 overpass leading into Needham begins the route with a good opportunity to get the blood flowing in your legs. Not to worry, though, you'll quickly be sailing down Greendale Avenue heading toward a nice multimile stretch along the rural atmosphere of South Street as you head into Dover.

Dover offers up two of the best stretches of road on the route. On the way out you'll ride a nearly 2-mile stretch along Claybrook Road, a virtually perfectly flat winding road that kicks up only at the end as you approach the Main Street crossing. On your return you'll enjoy a similar run along Pine Street. Though slightly uphill at times, this stretch is just as enjoyable but nearly twice as long as the one along Claybrook Road.

A large portion of the Needham Fitness Cruise encompasses a loop through Sherborn, a rural town with more than 50 percent of its area occupied by open space and no house-lot sizes less than a full acre of land. You'll soon discover how Forest Street is quite aptly named, and you'll also likely see a variety of animals in the area, from horses to llamas. You may even have to slow down or stop for a wild turkey in the road.

Miles and Directions

0.0 Nahanton Park.

0.1 Turn right onto Kendrick Street.

0.6 Turn left onto Hunting Road.

0.7 Road name changes to Greendale Avenue.

2.5 Turn right onto Great Plain Avenue.

2.6 Turn left onto South Street.

4.4 Bear left at intersection to remain on South Street.

5.9 Road name changes to Willow Street.

6.6 Turn right onto Cross Street (not marked). This is a sharp right before the stop sign. Don't go all the way to the stop sign.

7.0 Bear right onto Centre Street (not marked).

7.3 Turn left onto Claybrook Road.

9.4 Bear right onto Pleasant Street South.

10.0 Turn left onto Glen Street. Caution: This turn is at the bottom of a downhill on a fairly busy road with limited visibility of oncoming traffic.

12.3 Bear right onto Farm Street.

12.8 Turn right onto Bridge Street.

13.1 Road name changes to Farm Road.

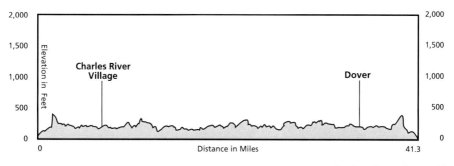

Needham Fitness Cruise

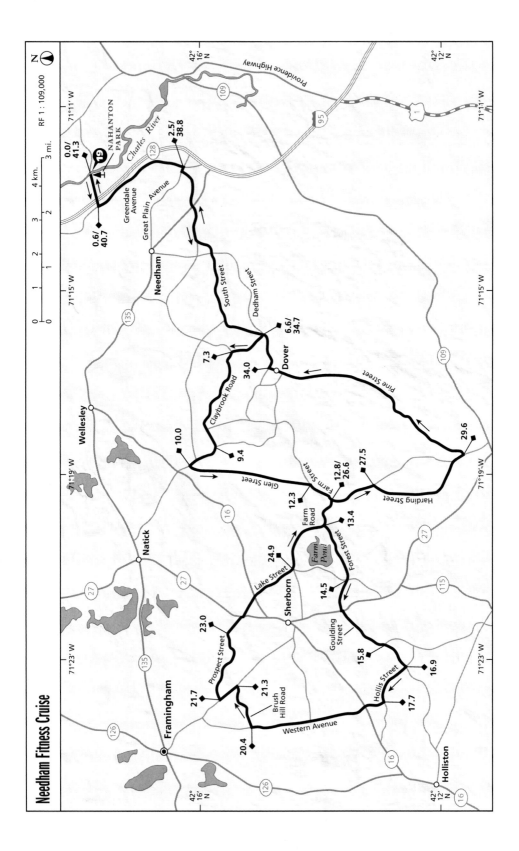

RF 1 : 109,000

13.4 Turn left onto Forest Street.

14.5 Bear right onto Goulding Street East.

15.2 Cross State Route 27 (South Main Street) onto Goulding Street West.

15.7 Bear right onto Woodland Street.

15.8 Bear left onto Mill Street.

16.9 Turn right onto Hollis Street.

17.7 Turn right onto Western Avenue.

20.4 Turn right onto Brush Hill Road.

21.3 Turn left onto Perry Street.

21.7 Turn right onto Prospect Street. Caution: Turn is sharp and is along the downhill section of Perry Street.

23.0 Turn right onto Coolidge Street.

23.4 Bear right onto SR 27 (North Main Street), then immediately bear left onto Lake Street.

24.9 Turn left onto Farm Road.

26.3 Road name changes to Bridge Street.

26.6 Turn right onto Farm Street.

27.5 Bear right onto Junction Street.

27.8 Road name changes to Harding Street.

29.4 Keep straight onto North Street.

29.6 Bear left onto Pine Street.

33.4 Bear right onto Centre Street.

33.9 Isabella's Groceria—food and drinks.

34.0 Keep right onto Dedham Street.

34.7 Turn left onto Willow Street.

35.4 Road name changes to South Street.

38.7 Turn right onto Great Plain Avenue.

38.8 Turn left onto Greendale Avenue.

40.6 Road name changes to Hunting Road.

40.7 Turn right at traffic light onto Kendrick Street.

41.3 Turn left immediately after bridge into Nahanton Park.

Ride Information

Local Information

Greater Boston Convention & Visitors Bureau, 2 Copley Place, Suite 105, Boston; (888) SEE-BOSTON, (617) 536-4100; www.boston usa.com.

Restaurants

Fava Restaurant, 1027 Great Plain Avenue, Needham; (781) 455-8668.

Accommodations

Sheraton, 100 Cabot Street, Needham; (781) 444-1110.

Green Suites International, 1038 Central Avenue, Needham; (781) 444-2878.

Map

DeLorme Massachusetts Atlas & Gazetteer, pages 40, 52.

20 Dover Cruise

Based on the popular In Search of the Llamas Charles River Wheelmen route, the Dover Cruise zigs and zags through quiet corners of Dover, Medfield, and Sherborn. You will likely see a variety of wildlife: horses, sheep, turkeys, and perhaps even llamas at Windy Knobb Farm, and pigs, ostrich, emu boars, and reindeer at Marino's Farm. The route contains many great low-traffic, tree-lined roads for cycling enjoyment. With no real climbs and plenty of opportunities for refreshments, this is a perfect cruising route just outside the Boston metropolitan area.

Start: Chickering Fields parking lot, across the street from Caryl Park on Dedham Street.
Length: 39.7 miles.
Ride time: 2.5 to 3 hours.
Terrain: Rolling and winding country roads.

Traffic and hazards: Low-traffic roads that are mostly in good condition. There are just a few short stints that involve crossings of busy roads.

Getting there: Take State Route 128 South to exit 17/State Route 135. Follow SR 135 West for about half a mile and turn left onto South Street. Follow for 1 mile and then turn left onto Chestnut Street. Merge onto Dedham Street and follow it for another 2 miles, and Chickering Fields parking lot will be on your right

Dover offers the best cycling roads in the vicinity of the SR 128 metropolitan Boston area. The Dover Cruise, based on the popular Charles River Wheelmen In Search of the Llamas ride, meanders through Dover and its closest peer in the area, Sherborn. Both towns are very rural, primarily residential towns, with working farms still representing the largest segment of the local economies. The Dover Cruise route will provide you with an opportunity to encounter a variety of wildlife on some of the area farms and the woodlands that line the route.

Heading through South Dover, you'll quickly find yourself cruising along Pine Street, a long and winding country road that goes on for miles, which is great fun on a bicycle. Next come the aptly named Farm and Forest Streets for more enjoyable cycling before you emerge in South Sherborn. Sherborn is a sparsely populated town where most house lots are an acre-plus and more than 50 percent of the town's land remains undeveloped, meaning more great cycling roads lie ahead.

From South Sherborn, you'll wind your way south toward Millis before heading back along Causeway Street, with its spectacular views of Windy Knobb Farm. The route takes a brief visit to the outskirts of Holliston for a convenient stop at the cyclist-friendly Coffee Haven for food and drinks.

The Dover Cruise leads you back through Sherborn and the north side of Dover, with a great run down Claybrook Road, a fun cycling road that winds alongside the Charles River. You will then pass through Dover Center with its spectacular views of the Charles River by the dam and Willow Street bridge, where more

Crane wading the Charles River, seen from Willow Street bridge in Dover

wildlife can usually be seen. Ducks like to swim in the calm waters behind the dam, and cranes and other more exotic wildlife have been spotted lurking in the area.

Miles and Directions

0.0 Turn right out of Chickering Fields parking lot onto Dedham Street.

0.1 Keep right onto Haven Street.

1.4 Keep straight onto Main Street.

2.0 Turn left onto Springdale Avenue. Caution: Oncoming traffic on Springdale Avenue only has a yield sign at this intersection.

2.9 Turn right onto Centre Street.

3.4 Turn left onto Pine Street.

6.7 Bear right onto Winter Street.

7.0 Turn left onto North Street (not marked).

7.1 Turn right onto Harding Street.

8.7 Road name changes to Junction Street.

9.0 Turn left onto Farm Street.

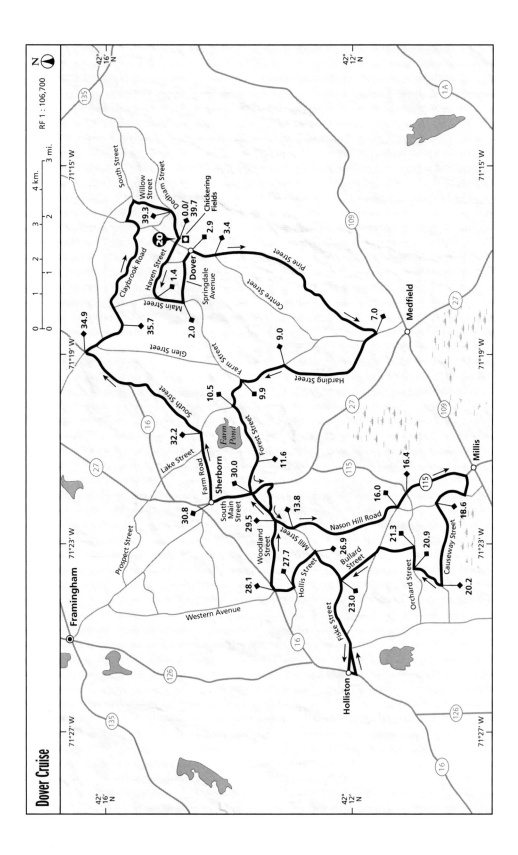

Dover Cruise

RF 1 : 106,700

N

9.9   Turn left onto Bridge Street. Caution: Limited visibility at bottom of hill.

10.2   Road name changes to Farm Road.

10.5   Turn left onto Forest Street.

11.6   Bear right onto Goulding Street (not marked). This turn is not marked and can be missed easily. It is a turn up a small hill to a stop sign. The street is marked at this intersection.

12.3   Turn left onto State Route 27 (South Main Street–not marked).

12.6   Keep right onto South Main Street.

12.7   Turn right onto Woodland Street.

13.4   Keep straight onto Mill Street.

13.8   Turn left onto Nason Hill Road.

15.5   Road name changes to Ridge Street.

16.0   Turn left onto Middlesex Street.

16.4   Keep straight onto State Route 115 (Exchange Street).

17.5   Bear right onto Curve Street (not marked) right after Little Peach convenience store.

17.7   Keep straight to stay on Curve Street.

17.9   Turn right onto Ridge Street.

18.6   Turn left onto Causeway Street (not marked).

20.2   Turn right onto Grove Street. Caution: This is a hairpin turn at the bottom of a hill, and Grove Street's pavement is very rough.

20.9   Turn right onto Orchard Street.

21.3   Turn left onto Bullard Lane.

22.0   Bear left onto Central Street.

22.1   Bear right onto Bullard Street.

23.0   Turn left onto Fiske Street.

24.5   Turn right onto Railroad Street.

24.6   Turn right onto Church Street.

24.8   Keep straight onto Central Street.

25.0   Keep left onto Fiske Street.

26.7   Road name changes to Mill Street.

26.9   Turn left onto Hollis Street.

27.7   Turn right onto Western Avenue.

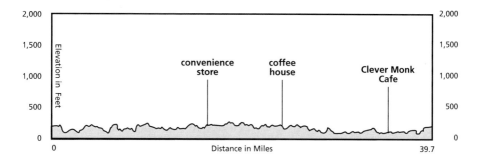

28.1 Turn right onto State Route 16 (Washington Street).

28.2 Keep right onto Woodland Street.

29.5 Bear left onto Goulding Street.

30.0 Turn left onto SR 27 (South Main Street—not marked).

30.8 Turn right onto Farm Road.

32.2 Turn left onto South Street.

33.9 Keep straight onto SR 16 (Eliot Street).

34.9 Bear right onto Mill Lane.

35.7 Bear left onto Claybrook Road.

37.8 Turn left onto Centre Street.

38.1 Turn right onto Fisher Street.

38.6 Road name changes to Willow Street.

39.3 Bear right onto Dedham Street.

39.7 Arrive back at Chickering Fields parking lot.

Ride Information

Local Information

Greater Boston Convention & Visitors Bureau, 2 Copley Place, Suite 105, Boston; (888) SEE-BOSTON, (617) 536-4100; www.boston usa.com.

Restaurants

Bubbling Brook Restaurant, 1652 High Street, Westwood; (781) 762-9860.

Clever Monk Cafe, 57 Eliot Street, Natick; (508) 655-4628.

Coffee Haven, 76 Railroad Street, Holliston; (508) 893-8075.

Accommodations

Sheraton, 100 Cabot Street, Needham; (781) 444-1110.

Green Suites International, 1038 Central Avenue, Needham; (781) 444-2878

Restrooms

0.0 Chickering Fields parking lot, portable toilet.

Map

DeLorme Massachusetts Atlas & Gazetteer, pages 40, 52.

21 Hingham Ramble

This ride explores Hingham, the first town southeast of Boston that is spaciously and graciously suburban rather than congested. It is an affluent community graced with elegant wooden homes from the early 1800s, horse farms, country estates with gently rolling meadows, and a beautiful stretch of waterfront along Massachusetts Bay. Hingham is unique because it has two centers of town, Hingham and Hingham Center, a mile apart. Both are New England classics, with proud old churches and fine colonial-style homes with peaked roofs and dormer windows.

Start: Burger King on State Route 228 at the Rockland-Norwell town line, immediately north of State Route 3.
Length: 22.5 miles.
Ride time: 1.5 hours.

Terrain: Gently rolling, with a few short, steep hills.
Traffic and hazards: Mostly quiet roads, though Main Street Hingham can be busy at times.

Getting there: Take SR 3 to exit 14 and follow SR 228 to Burger King.

Starting from the southern edge of the town, the ride heads north to the ocean at Crow Point, where you'll climb a short hill with a glorious view of Massachusetts Bay and the Boston skyline in the distance. You'll follow the waterfront and then head south for about 2 miles to the handsome center of town. Here you'll pass the Old Ship Church, built in 1681, the oldest church in America in continuous use.

The route now heads to World's End, as idyllic a spot as any on the Massachusetts coast. It is a small peninsula originally landscaped by Frederick Law Olmsted and now maintained by the Trustees of Reservations. It contains three drumlins, with a narrow neck between the first and second. Broad, grassy slopes lined with stately rows of trees slant gently down to the shore and give views of the Boston skyline. It's about a 3-mile loop on dirt roads to the far end of the peninsula; you may either ride or walk. The nonmembers entrance fee is currently $4.50.

After leaving World's End, you'll ride through Hingham Center, the older and less commercial of the two centers of town. The last part of the ride, south of Hingham Center, leads into a pastoral landscape of meticulous gentleman farms with broad fields and gracious old farmhouses.

Miles and Directions

0.0 Depart Burger King on SR 228, left heading toward SR 3.
0.1 Turn right onto Gardner Street.
2.6 Turn left onto SR 228 (Main Street).
5.4 Turn left onto Cedar Street.

Summer Street, Hingham

5.5 Bear right onto Hersey Street.

6.6 Road name changes to Thaxter Street.

7.2 Road name changes to Downer Avenue.

8.4 Road name changes to Malcolm Street.

8.6 Road name changes to Howe Street.

8.7 Turn right onto Jarvis Avenue.

8.9 Bear left onto Westview Circle, then immediately turn right onto Bel Air Road.

9.5 Turn right onto Park Circle.

9.7 Keep right onto Planters Field Lane.

9.9 Bear right onto Downer Avenue.

10.2 Road name changes to Thaxter Street.

10.8 Turn left onto North Street.

11.2 Turn right onto Main Street.

12.2 Turn left onto SR 228 (Short Street).

12.3 Bear right onto SR 228 (Leavitt Street).

12.4 Keep straight onto SR 228 (East Street).

13.1 Turn left onto Summer Street.

13.7 Bear right onto Martins Lane.

14.4 Entrance to World's End. Turn around.

14.6 Turn right onto Martins Cove Road.

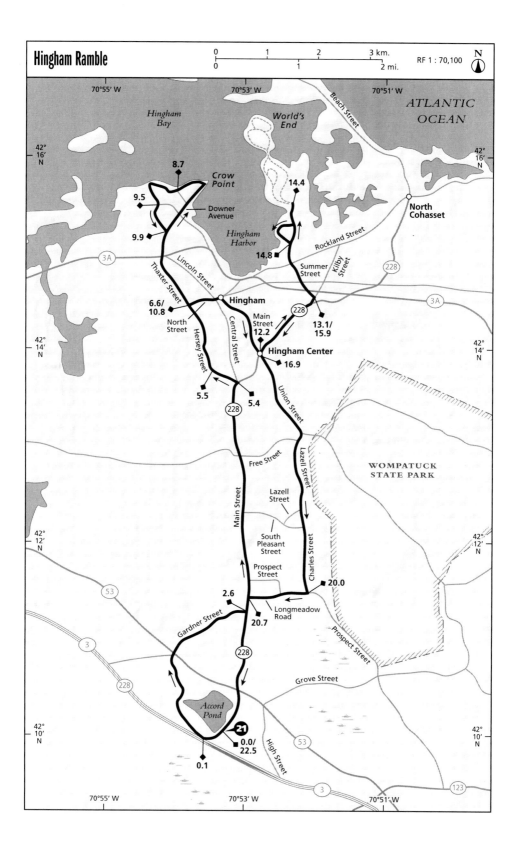

Hingham Ramble

0   1   2   3 km.

0   1   2 mi.

RF 1 : 70,100

N

70°55' W   70°53' W   70°51' W

Hingham Bay

World's End

Beach Street

ATLANTIC OCEAN

42° 16' N

42° 16' N

8.7

Crow Point

14.4

9.5

Downer Avenue

North Cohasset

9.9

Hingham Harbor

Rockland Street

3A

Lincoln Street

14.8

Summer Street

Kilby Street

228

Thaxter Street

6.6/ 10.8

Hersey Street

Central Street

Hingham

Main Street

12.2

228

13.1/ 15.9

3A

North Street

42° 14' N

42° 14' N

Hingham Center

16.9

5.5

5.4

228

Union Street

Free Street

Lazell Street

WOMPATUCK STATE PARK

Main Street

Lazell Street

Charles Street

South Pleasant Street

42° 12' N

42° 12' N

Prospect Street

20.0

53

2.6

Longmeadow Road

Gardner Street

20.7

Prospect Street

228

Grove Street

3

228

Accord Pond

42° 10' N

21

53

42° 10' N

0.0/ 22.5

High Street

0.1

123

70°55' W   70°53' W   70°51' W

3

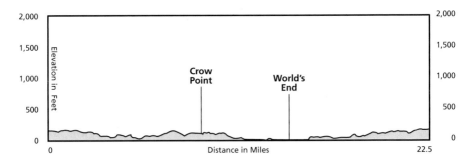

14.8 Turn right onto Seal Cove Road.

15.1 Turn right onto Martins Lane.

15.3 Bear left onto Summer Street.

15.9 Turn right onto SR 228 (East Street).

16.6 Keep straight onto SR 228 (Leavitt Street).

16.8 Bear left onto SR 228 (Short Street).

16.9 Turn left onto Middle Street.

17.2 Road name changes to Union Street.

18.0 Keep straight onto Lazell Street.

18.9 Keep straight onto Charles Street.

20.0 Turn right onto Prospect Street.

20.3 Turn left onto Longmeadow Road.

20.7 Turn left onto SR 228 (Main Street).

22.5 Arrive back at Burger King.

Ride Information

Local Information

Greater Boston Convention & Visitors Bureau, 2 Copley Place, Suite 105, Boston; (888) SEE-BOSTON, (617) 536-4100; www.boston usa.com.

Local Events and Attractions

The Trustees of Reservations, 227 East Street, Hingham; (781) 740-7233. World's End, Weir River Farm, Whitney and Thayer Woods.

Restaurants

Chili's Grill & Bar, 6 Whiting Street, Hingham; (781) 740-1313.

Panera Bread, 92 Derby Street, Hingham; (781) 740-2550.

Accommodations

Bare Cove B&B, 235 Rockland Street, Hingham; (781) 740-1422.

Cohasset Harbor Resort, 124 Elm Street, Cohasset; (781) 383-6650.

Super 8 Motel, 655 Washington Street, Weymouth; (781) 337-5200.

Restrooms

0.0 Burger King

Map

DeLorme Massachusetts Atlas & Gazetteer, pages 42, 54.

22 Cohasset Coastal Ramble

The Cohasset Coastal Ramble explores the shoulder of land southeast of Boston where the coastline curves primarily from an east-west to a north-south direction. It is the first really nice stretch of coast heading southeast from the city, and the Cohasset section, just east of Hull, is among the most scenic in the state. A network of smooth secondary roads connecting these two affluent communities provides bicycling at its best.

Start: Cohasset Junior-Senior High School on Pond Street, Cohasset.
Length: 26.8 miles.
Ride time: 2 hours.
Terrain: Gently rolling, with a couple of short hills.

Traffic and hazards: Quiet roads along private beaches, which remain quiet even during the summer.

Getting there: From State Route 3, take exit 14 and follow State Route 228 North toward Hingham. Follow for 6.5 miles and then take a right onto State Route 3A. Follow for 2.7 miles, take a left at the traffic light onto Pond Street, and travel 0.2 mile to Cohasset Junior-Senior High School.

The ride starts in Cohasset, an unspoiled community that is one of the finest of the Boston suburbs. Its splendid rocky coastline, rimmed by large, impressive homes hovering above the waves with the Boston skyline in the distance rivals Cape Ann and Newport for elegance. The center of town is a New England jewel, with a long, stately green framed by a pair of graceful white churches, the town hall, and fine colonial-style wooden homes. The church at the head of the green was built in 1747. Cohasset received a burst of publicity in 1986 when much of the movie *The Witches of Eastwick* was filmed here.

The ride continues southeast into Scituate, another handsome community with a large green, a small, boat-filled harbor, and a compact row of shops along its shore. Just outside of town is the Lawson Tower, a handsome wooden-shingled landmark with a water tower inside. It was built in 1902 and given to the town by Thomas Lawson, a copper magnate. At the top is a set of bells that are played on special town occasions. The Scituate coast is bordered by smaller homes and cottages. It is spectacular, especially on a windy day when the surf crashes against the seawalls, which are necessary to protect the shore from the brunt of northeasters. There's a graceful white lighthouse at the tip of Cedar Point, and the bridge over the tidal inlet that forms the border of the two towns is a great spot to view the coastline.

Cohasset Coastal Ramble

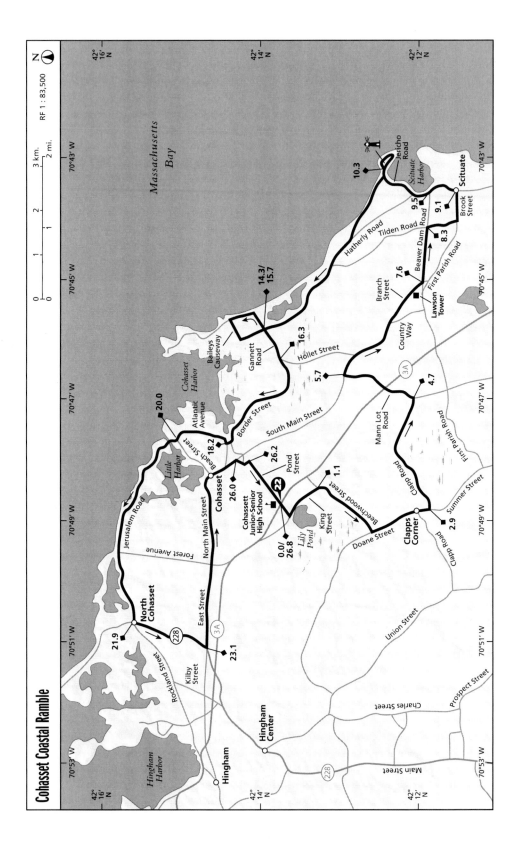

RF 1 : 83,500

Scituate Harbor

Miles and Directions

0.0 Depart Cohasset Junior-Senior High School, 143 Pond Street, Cohasset.

0.5 Turn left onto King Street.

1.1 Turn right onto Beechwood Street.

2.2 Turn left onto Church Street.

2.4 Road name changes to Summer Street.

2.9 Turn left onto Thomas Clapp Road.

4.7 Road name changes to Mann Lot Road.

5.7 Turn right onto Country Way.

6.8 Keep straight onto Branch Street.

7.6 Bear left onto Beaver Dam Road.

8.3 Turn right onto Tilden Road.

8.7 Road name changes to Brook Street.

9.1 Turn left onto Front Street.

9.4 Road name changes to Beaver Dam Road.

9.5 Turn right onto Jericho Road.

10.3 Bear right onto Lighthouse Road.

10.7 Road name changes to Rebecca Road.

11.1 Turn right onto Lighthouse Road.

11.2 Keep right onto Turner Road.

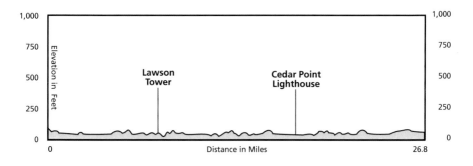

11.8 Turn right onto Hatherly Road.

14.3 Turn right onto Gannett Road.

14.6 Road name changes to Glades Road.

14.9 Turn left onto Bailey's Causeway.

15.3 Road name changes to Hatherly Road.

15.7 Turn right onto Gannett Road.

16.3 Turn right onto Border Street.

17.9 Turn right onto Margin Street.

18.2 Road name changes to Atlantic Avenue.

20.0 Bear right onto Jerusalem Road.

21.9 Turn left onto SR 228 (Hull Street).

23.1 Take a sharp left onto East Street.

23.6 Road name changes to North Main Street.

26.0 Turn right onto Spring Street.

26.2 Turn left to stay on Spring Street, go 100 yards and turn right onto Pond Street.

26.8 Arrive back at Cohasset Junior-Senior High School.

Ride Information

Local Information

Greater Boston Convention & Visitors Bureau, 2 Copley Place, Suite 105, Boston; (888) SEE-BOSTON, (617) 536-4100; www.boston usa.com.

Restaurants

Papa Gino's: Cohasset Plaza, 380 Chief Justice Cushing Highway, Cohasset; (781) 383-6303.

Red Lion Inn Restaurant, 71 South Main Street, Cohasset; (781) 383-1704.

Accommodations

Cohasset Harbor Resort, 124 Elm Street, Cohasset; (781) 383-6650.

Red Lion Inn Resort, 71 South Main Street, Cohasset; (781) 383-1704.

Super 8 Motel, 655 Washington Street, Weymouth, (781) 337-5200.

Map

DeLorme Massachusetts Atlas & Gazetteer, pages 42, 54.

23 South Shore Coastal Cruise

Convenient to Boston, the South Shore Coastal Cruise explores the quiet, tree-lined streets of the city's southern coastal suburbs along with their wealth of stunning coastline roads. Almost half of the route is along the Atlantic coast with spectacular views of the ocean and the rocky coastline, complete with visits to lighthouses, beaches, and a windmill. Enjoy a unique view of the Boston skyline from Pemberton Point in Hull and the serenity of Wompatuck State Park in Hingham, which is named for an Indian chief the local colonists knew as Josiah Wompatuck, on this flat and very enjoyable half-century route.

Start: Park'n'ride lot, Rockland (opposite Home Depot).
Length: 52.7 miles.
Ride time: 3 to 3.5 hours.

Terrain: Mostly flat with a few small hills. Many scenic miles along the Atlantic coast.
Traffic and hazards: State Route 228 can be busy

Getting there: Take State Route 3 to exit 14 (SR 228) in Rockland. Turn left at the end of the ramp, then left again at the first set of lights, and park in the Park'n'ride lot.

The South Shore Coastal Cruise is a gem of a half-century located just outside of Boston. The convenient start just off SR 3 is somewhat misleading, as you will soon leave all things metropolitan behind. Within a few miles, you enter Wompatuck State Park, one of the only hilly sections along the route, which serves to slow you down and encourages you to relax and enjoy the serenity of this wonderful natural resource.

Named after a local Indian chief known to colonists as Josiah Wompatuck who deeded the park and surrounding lands to colonists in 1665, the park would later be used as a munitions depot by the U.S. Army during World War II. The park also has a rich cycling history, as the Mass Bay Road Club has hosted a twice-weekly bicycle training race series within the park for many years. This is a great chance to see local pros or to try some racing yourself along a safe and fun closed course.

Your first ocean view comes at Scituate Harbor, with dozens of boats moored in its calm water. A loop around Cedar Point will take you to the Scituate Lighthouse, a 50-foot tower built in 1811, before heading up to North Scituate Beach for another quick loop out along Glades Road for a great view of Massachusetts Bay. After these quick peeks, you'll enjoy a 3-mile ride along the coast as you proceed down Atlantic Avenue and Jerusalem Road, passing Quarry Point and Sandy Beach in Cohasset.

There are more stunning ocean views to be had, as you'll find along the next segment of the ride up the Hull peninsula. The South Shore Coastal Cruise takes

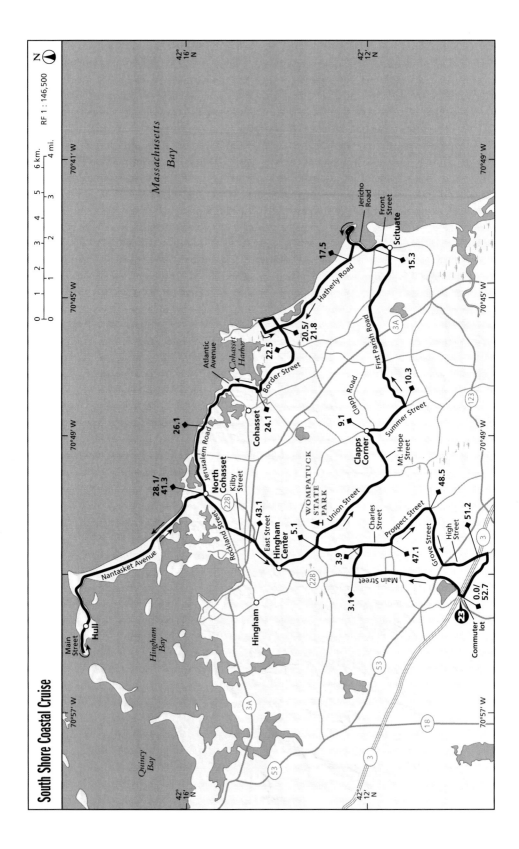

South Shore Coastal Cruise

RF 1 : 146,500

N

you along Nantasket Beach and out to Pemberton Point, with a stop at Fort Revere Park, where you can climb the tower for a 360-degree panoramic view of Hingham Bay, Quincy Bay, Boston Harbor, and Massachusetts Bay. The tower is open only on weekends and holidays between May and September; check with park staff at (617) 727–4468 for specific details. From the fort, you'll meander through Hull out to Pemberton Point and the site of the Hull Windmill, which generates electrical power for Hull High School, also located on Pemberton Point. Here you can view the Boston skyline and Logan Airport across the bay before you head back along the peninsula and into Hingham.

A final bit of climbing past Wompatuck State Park will bring you back to the ride start, where you'll likely be anxious to start planning your next ride along the South Shore Coastal Cruise route. This is one of my personal favorite rides and kudos must be given to the Charles River Wheelmen once again, as the route is based on their popular Sunday Morning Fitness Ride—South Shore Coastal Loop, led by Andy Brand and Bob Dyson.

Miles and Directions

0.0 Take a left out of the commuter parking lot onto SR 228.

3.1 Turn right onto South Pleasant Street.

3.9 Bear left onto Charles Street.

4.2 Keep straight onto Lazell Street.

5.1 Turn right onto Union Street into Wampatuck State Park.

7.6 Exit the park through the gate, which likely will be closed. Road name changes to Mt. Blue Street here.

7.7 Turn left onto Mt. Hope Street.

8.3 Road name changes to Thomas Clapp Road.

9.1 Turn right onto Summer Street.

10.3 Turn left onto First Parish Road.

14.8 Turn left onto Front Street.

15.2 Road name changes to Beaver Dam Road.

15.3 Turn right onto Jericho Road.

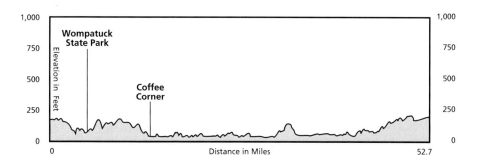

16.0 Bear right onto Lighthouse Road.

16.5 Road name changes to Rebecca Road.

16.9 Turn right onto Lighthouse Road.

17.0 Bear left onto Jericho Road.

17.5 Turn right onto Hatherly Road.

20.5 Turn right onto Gannett Road.

20.7 Road name changes to Glades Road.

21.1 Turn left onto Bailey's Causeway.

21.4 Road name changes to Hatherly Road.

21.8 Turn right onto Gannett Road.

22.5 Turn right onto Border Street.

24.1 Bear right at fork, follow for 50 yards, turn right onto Margin Street.

24.4 Road name changes to Atlantic Avenue.

26.1 Bear right onto Jerusalem Road.

28.1 Turn right onto SR 228 (Hull Street).

28.2 Bear left onto SR 228 (Nantasket Avenue).

29.3 Keep right onto Nantasket Avenue.

29.6 Turn left onto Water Street, then immediately turn left onto Nantasket Avenue.

29.9 Bear right onto George Washington Boulevard, follow for 150 yards then bear left at the fork to connect to Nantasket Avenue.

30.0 Bear left onto Nantasket Avenue.

32.7 Bear left onto Fitzpatrick Way.

33.2 Bear left onto Nantasket Avenue.

33.5 Keep right to stay on Nantasket Avenue.

34.0 Turn left onto Farina Road.

34.5 Bear left onto Nantasket Avenue, then immediately turn right onto Spring Street.

34.8 Road name changes to Ocean Avenue. Turn around

35.0 Turn right onto Main Street.

36.1 Keep straight onto Spring Street.

36.6 Keep straight onto Nantasket Avenue.

36.9 Bear right onto Fitzpatrick Way.

37.4 Bear right onto Nantasket Avenue.

40.1 Keep left onto SR 228 (Nantasket Avenue).

41.3 Bear left onto SR 228 (Hull Street), then immediately turn right onto Rockland Street.

42.3 Bear left onto Kilby Street.

43.1 Bear right onto SR 228 (East Street).

43.7 Turn left onto Spring Street.

44.0 Bear left onto School Street.

44.2 Turn right onto Pleasant Street.

45.0 Keep straight onto Lazell Street.

46.0 Keep straight onto Charles Street.

47.1 Turn left onto Prospect Street.

48.5 Turn right onto Grove Street.

50.0 Road name changes to High Street.

51.2 Turn right onto Longwater Drive.

51.5 Turn right to stay on Longwater Drive.

52.4 Bear right onto Pond Street.

52.6 Turn left onto SR 228 (Hingham Street).

52.7 Arrive back at commuter parking lot.

Ride Information

Local Information

Greater Boston Convention & Visitors Bureau, 2 Copley Place, Suite 105, Boston; (888) SEE-BOSTON, (617) 536-4100; www.boston usa.com.

Local Events and Attractions

Wompatuck Criterium Training Series, Mass Bay Road Club, P.O. Box 791, Plymouth, MA 02362; www.massbayroadclub.org. Held mid-April through August on Tuesday and Wednesday evenings.

Restaurants

Papa Gino's: Cohasset Plaza, 380 Chief Justice Cushing Highway, Cohasset; (781) 383-6303.

Red Lion Inn Restaurant, 71 South Main Street, Cohasset; (781) 383-1704.

Accommodations

Cohasset Harbor Resort, 124 Elm Street, Cohasset; (781) 383-6650.

Red Lion Inn Resort, 71 South Main Street, Cohasset; (781) 383-1704.

Super 8 Motel, 655 Washington Street, Weymouth, (781) 337-5200.

Map

DeLorme Massachusetts Atlas & Gazetteer, pages 42, 54.

24 Plymouth Cruise

The Plymouth Cruise is a tour of Plymouth and the scrub-pine and cranberry-bog country surrounding it. You'll go past or near many of the town's historic landmarks. Outside of town you'll go through the Myles Standish State Forest, a large, unspoiled area of pines and ponds. The cranberry-growing area is a uniquely beautiful part of the state to explore by bicycle, especially during the harvest season in October when the berries turn the bogs into a crimson carpet. Surrounded by pines and sandy banks, with little wooden sheds next to them, the bogs have a trim, rustic appeal. Narrow roads guide the bicyclist from bog to bog past cedar-shingled homes.

Start: Shaw's Supermarket, Plymouth.
Length: 28.6 miles.
Ride time: 2 hours.

Terrain: Gently rolling, with a few short hills.
Traffic and hazards: Nice quiet roads.

Getting there: Take exit 6B off of State Route 3 and follow U.S. Route 44 0.4 mile west to Pilgrim Hill Road. Turn left at the traffic light onto Pilgrim Hill Road and park in Shaw's parking lot.

You'll start the ride by visiting the Pilgrim Monument, a soaring Victorian granite statue built in 1889. From here it's just a couple of blocks to the waterfront, where you'll go by Cranberry World, a museum of the cranberry and the cranberry industry. It's free and worth seeing. Just ahead is Plymouth Bay Winery, which manufactures and sells wine from locally grown grapes and cranberries. Stop in for a taste of cranberry wine. A little farther along the waterfront are the *Mayflower II* and Plymouth Rock. When you see the *Mayflower II,* you'll be surprised at how small it is. Plymouth Rock, despite its historic significance, is just a plain old rock covered by an ornate pillared portico. Within a couple of blocks are numerous other attractions and historic buildings, including a wax museum depicting Pilgrim life; the Federal-era Antiquarian House; and the outstanding Pilgrim Hall Museum, one of the oldest in the country, founded in 1824. It contains extensive displays of Pilgrim possessions and artifacts.

Leaving Plymouth you'll head to the Myles Standish State Forest, an extensive wilderness area of scrub pine spreading up and over an endless succession of bubblelike little hills and hollows. Biking through this terrain is a lot of fun if you use your gears properly, roller-coastering down one little hill and over the next one. Several small ponds lie nestled in the pines. Beyond the forest you abruptly enter cranberry-bog country. You'll go through a long string of bogs and pass near Savery Avenue, the first divided highway in America, built in 1861. The road consists of two narrow lanes with pine trees between them and on each side, extending a half mile alongside State Route 58.

Massachusetts Bay

Miles and Directions

0.0 Depart Shaw's Supermarket, 10 Pilgrim Hill Road, Plymouth.

0.2 Turn left onto Summer Street.

1.1 Turn left onto Oak Street.

1.5 Turn right onto US 44 (Samoset Street).

1.6 Turn left onto Allerton Street.

2.0 Turn right onto State Route 3A (Court Street), then immediately turn left onto Lothrop Street.

2.2 Turn right onto Water Street.

2.9 Bear right onto Leyden Street.

3.0 Turn left onto to Market Street.

3.1 Bear right onto Summer Street.

3.5 Keep left onto Billington Street.

3.7 Keep left to stay on Billington Street.

5.6 Road name changes to Watercourse Road.

6.1 Road name changes to Rocky Pond Road.

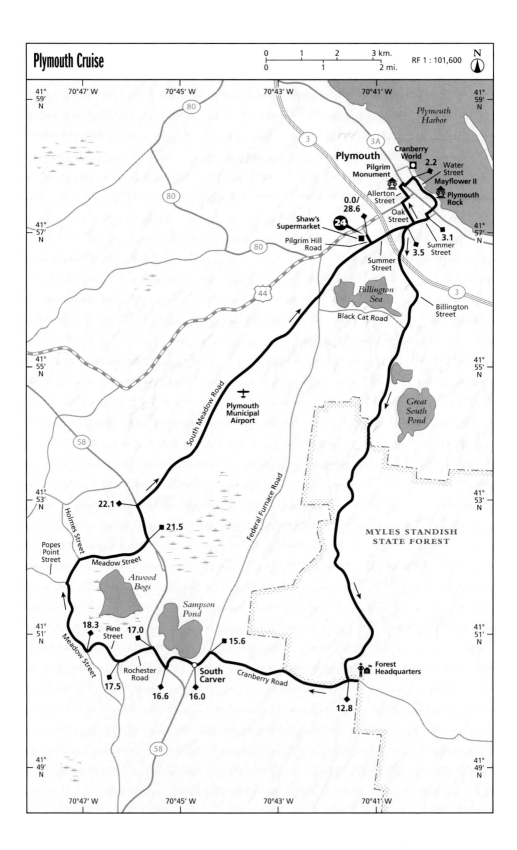

Plymouth Cruise

0   1   2   3 km.

0   1   2 mi.

RF 1 : 101,600

N

41° 59' N

70°47' W

70°45' W

70°43' W

70°41' W

41° 59' N

Plymouth Harbor

80

3

3A

Plymouth

Cranberry World

2.2

Water Street

Pilgrim Monument

Mayflower II

80

Allerton Street

0.0/ 28.6

Plymouth Rock

41° 57' N

Shaw's Supermarket

Oak Street

24

3.1

Summer Street

80

Pilgrim Hill Road

3.5

41° 57' N

Summer Street

Billington Sea

Billington Street

44

Black Cat Road

3

41° 55' N

Plymouth Municipal Airport

Great South Pond

41° 55' N

58

Federal Furnace Road

41° 53' N

22.1

MYLES STANDISH STATE FOREST

41° 53' N

21.5

Holmes Street

Popes Point Street

Meadow Street

Atwood Bogs

41° 51' N

18.3

Pine Street

Sampson Pond

Meadow Street

17.0

15.6

Forest Headquarters

41° 51' N

Rochester Road

South Carver

Cranberry Road

17.5

16.6

16.0

12.8

41° 49' N

58

41° 49' N

70°47' W

70°45' W

70°43' W

70°41' W

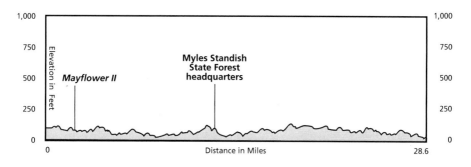

7.9 Turn right to stay on Rocky Pond Road.

8.6 Bear left onto Bare Hill Road.

11.6 Keep straight onto Lower College Pond Road.

12.8 Turn right onto Cranberry Road.

15.6 Turn left onto Tremont Street.

16.0 Bear right onto Lakeview Street.

16.6 Bear right onto SR 58 (South Main Street).

17.0 Turn left onto Rochester Road.

17.5 Keep right onto Pine Street.

17.8 Keep right to stay on Pine Street.

18.3 Bear right onto Meadow Street.

21.5 Turn left onto SR 58 (Main Street).

22.1 Turn right onto South Meadow Road.

27.0 Bear left onto Federal Furnace Road.

27.9 Road name changes to Summer Street.

28.3 Turn left onto Pilgrim Hill Road.

28.6 Arrive back at Shaw's.

Ride Information

Local Information

Plymouth County Convention & Visitors Bureau, 32 Court Street, 2nd Floor, Plymouth; (800) 231-1620, (508) 747-0100; www.see plymouth.com.

Restaurants

Carver Gas & Convenience Store, 224 Tremont Street, Carver; (508) 866-4795.

Pizza Factory, 4 Pilgrim Hill Road, Plymouth; (508) 747-7474.

Accommodations

John Carver Inn, 25 Summer Street, Plymouth; (508) 746-7100.

Radisson Hotel, 180 Water Street, Plymouth; (508) 747-4900.

Restrooms

2.8 Plymouth Rock.

12.0 Myles Standish.

Map

DeLorme Massachusetts Atlas & Gazetteer, page 58.

25 Cape in a Day Classic

An ambitious double-metric century ride from downtown Boston to the very tip of Cape Cod, the Cape in a Day Classic is not for the fainthearted. The only "one-way" ride in this book, you must plan carefully to tackle this one. You'll need to leave by the break of daylight to ensure you make it to Provincetown in time to catch the ferry back to Boston. If you make it, you will have earned bragging rights to a classic Massachusetts ride challenge. If you don't, you'll get to spend some extra time in one of the Cape's quaint, out-of-the-way towns. Invite some friends along to share this unique cycling experience and also to help ensure a safe trip. Don't go it alone. Also keep in mind that the *Provincetown II* ferry runs only on Saturdays and Sundays from late June to early September. Check with the Bay State Cruise Company (617–748–1428) for specific details.

Start: Black Falcon Terminal, South Boston.
Length: 124.2 miles.
Ride time: 8 to 10 hours. Plan carefully!
Terrain: Rolling hills with some short, steep climbs.
Traffic and hazards: You must depart Boston very early to avoid traffic in town and along State Route 3A. Care must be taken on the short stretch along U.S. Route 6, a very busy road with a wide shoulder. This is a long, challenging ride, and as such it should be attempted only with a group of experienced and fit cyclists.

Getting there: Travel Interstate 93 South to exit 23, and take an immediate left onto Seaport Boulevard. Follow to end of road (name changes to Northern Avenue) and take a right and another immediate right. You are now at the Black Falcon terminal; this is where the ferry is going to drop you off at the end of the ride. You can park in the five-story garage for $12, any of the other lots in the area, or along the street. Be sure to know where you park in relation to the terminal, so you can find your way back to the car at the end of the ride.

The challenge of riding the Cape in a Day has long been a goal of avid cyclists in Massachusetts. In fact, it is a version of this challenge that inspired Billy Starr to develop the Pan Mass Challenge (PMC) bike-a-thon, the country's most successful sports fund-raiser. Now more than twenty-six years old, the Pan Mass Challenge has raised 145 million-plus dollars for cancer research. The PMC served as my personal inspiration not only for fund-raising for cancer research but also for cycling. If you're inspired to embark on this challenge, you'll feel energized when it is complete, as it's quite an accomplishment.

As you prepare to depart South Boston, soak in the wonderful views of the sunrise in Massachusetts Bay, giving life to a new day across the Boston skyline. You really do need to see the sun rise over Boston to do this ride right. You've only got until 3:00 P.M. to buy your ticket and board the *Provincetown II* ferry some 124 miles away if you hope to see the Boston skyline again today.

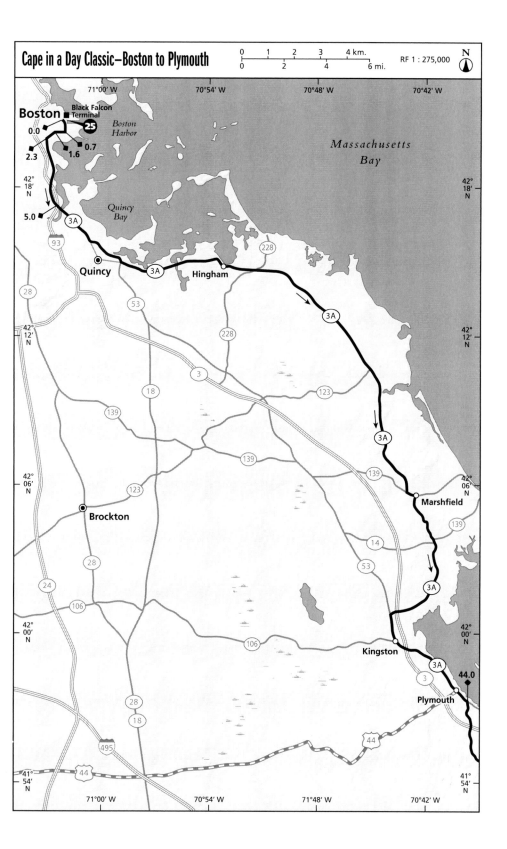

Cape in a Day Classic—Boston to Plymouth

0	1	2	3	4 km.

| 0 | | 2 | | 4 | | 6 mi. |

RF 1 : 275,000

N

Boston

Black Falcon Terminal

25

0.0

Boston Harbor

0.7

2.3

1.6

Massachusetts Bay

42° 18' N

42° 18' N

Quincy Bay

5.0

3A

93

Quincy

3A

Hingham

228

228

53

3A

42° 12' N

42° 12' N

3

18

139

123

3A

123

139

28

139

42° 06' N

42° 06' N

123

Brockton

3A

Marshfield

14

28

139

53

24

3A

106

42° 00' N

42° 00' N

106

Kingston

3A

28

3

44.0

18

Plymouth

495

44

44

41° 54' N

41° 54' N

71°00' W

70°54' W

71°48' W

70°42' W

Cape in a Day Classic—Plymouth to Yarmouth

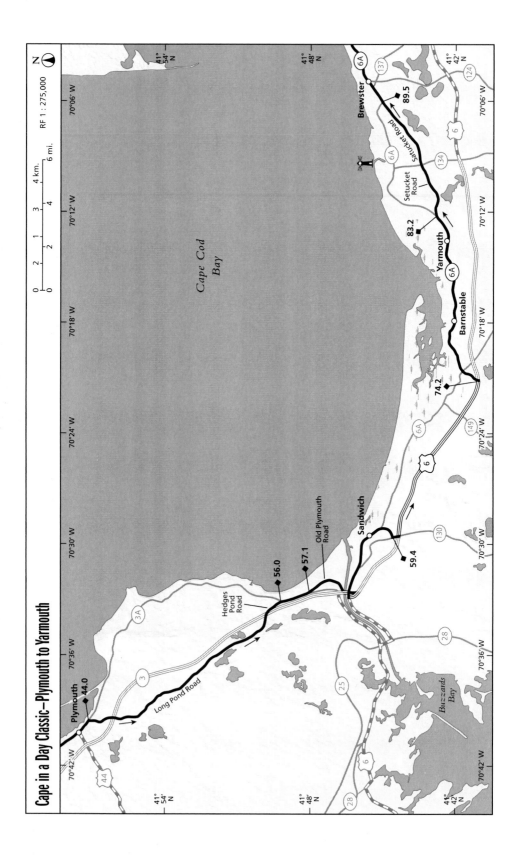

RF 1 : 275,000

N

Plymouth **◆ 44.0**

Long Pond Road

Hedges Pond Road

◆ 56.0

◆ 57.1

Old Plymouth Road

Sandwich

■ 59.4

130

◆ 74.2

Barnstable

6A

149

6

Yarmouth

■ 83.2

Setucket Road

Sandwich Road

134

6

■ 89.5

Brewster

6A

137

124

Cape Cod Bay

Buzzards Bay

3A

3

25

28

44

6

28

70°42' W
70°36' W
70°30' W
70°24' W
70°18' W
70°12' W
70°06' W

41°54' N
41°48' N
41°42' N

0 1 2 3 4 5 6 mi.
0 2 4 6 km.

Coast Guard fireboat in Boston Harbor

Wind your way through the quiet early morning streets of South Boston and the heavily developed areas of Quincy and Hingham, with great views of Quincy Bay and Hingham Bay. Massachusetts Bay pops into view again in Marshfield Hills and Plymouth, a key point along Christopher Columbus's own spectacular journey. While you've mostly followed SR 3A to this point, be sure not to follow it out of Plymouth. The route takes a turn along South Street out of Plymouth and winds down a variety of back roads to the Sagamore Bridge.

The Public Works Administration, born out of relief efforts of the Great Depression, began constructing the Sagamore Bridge (and its sister bridge in Bourne) in 1933, replacing three smaller problematic bridges that spanned the Cape Cod Canal. In accordance with Public Works Administration regulations, work was distributed widely, and, wherever practical, hand labor was used instead of machinery to provide as many jobs as possible. You'll now cross this magnificent work to officially begin your ride up the full length of Cape Cod. Be sure to walk your bike along the sidewalk of the bridge and use extreme caution both getting on and off.

After cruising through Sandwich on State Route 6A, the road diverges to the cycling friendly service road that runs alongside US 6. With hardly any traffic to

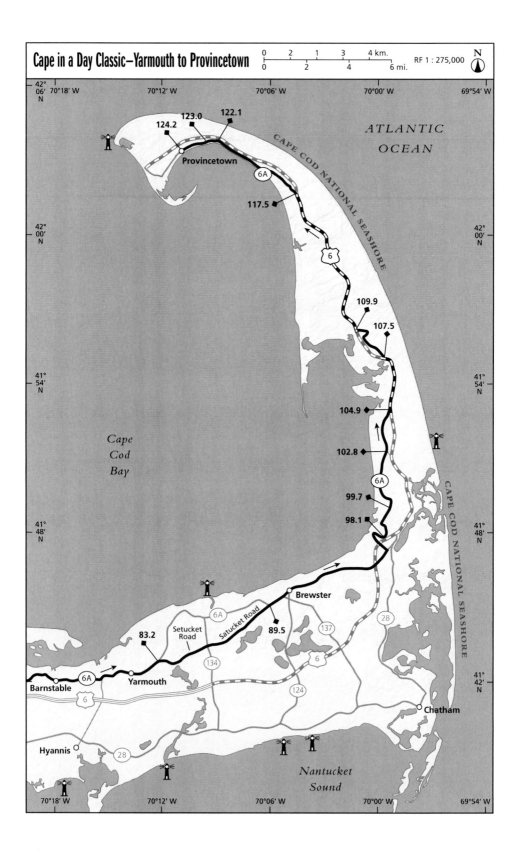

Cape in a Day Classic—Yarmouth to Provincetown

RF 1 : 275,000

N

0   2   1   3   4 km.
0   2   4   6 mi.

ATLANTIC OCEAN

CAPE COD NATIONAL SEASHORE

Provincetown

124.2
123.0
122.1
117.5
6A
6
109.9
107.5
104.9
102.8
6A
99.7
98.1

Cape Cod Bay

Brewster

Setucket Road
Satucket Road
89.5
83.2

6A
28
137
6
124
134

Barnstable
Yarmouth
6

CAPE COD NATIONAL SEASHORE

Chatham

Hyannis

28

Nantucket Sound

42°06' N
70°18' W   70°12' W   70°06' W   70°00' W   69°54' W

42°00' N

41°54' N

41°48' N

41°42' N

bother you, you can enjoy the rolling hills along these quiet wooded roads. You'll pop back out to SR 6A again in Barnstable for an enjoyable ride along the northern side of the Cape, passing through a variety of quaint towns with many nice spots to stop for coffee or food. You'll wind your way through Eastham and then need to ride several miles along the busy US 6 in order to make it to the outer reaches of the Cape. The shoulder is wide, but traffic can get very busy along US 6. Use caution.

Finally, you'll emerge in Provincetown, a bustling community on the very tip of Cape Cod. Make your way down to the chamber of commerce on Commercial Street and get your ticket for the ferry (current price is $18). Be sure to buy for your bike too (currently priced at $5.00). The ferry begins boarding at 3:00 P.M. and departs at 3:30 P.M., arriving back at Black Falcon terminal in Boston around 6:30 P.M. Whew!

Miles and Directions

0.0   Depart Pete's Dockside.

0.6   Road name changes to L Street.

0.7   Turn right onto East Broadway.

1.2   Road name changes to Dorchester Street.

1.6   Bear left onto Old Colony Avenue.

2.2   Keep straight onto Columbia Road.

2.3   At roundabout, take the second exit onto Morrissey Boulevard (William T. Morrissey Boulevard).

5.0   Turn left onto Neponset Avenue.

5.1   Road name changes to SR 3A (Neponset Avenue).

5.2   Road name changes to Neponset Bridge.

5.4   Keep left onto Quincy Shore Drive.

5.6   Bear right onto ramp.

5.7   Turn left onto Commander Shea Boulevard.

5.8   Take ramp (right) onto SR 3A (Hancock Street).

7.5   Keep straight onto Hancock Street.

8.4   After passing Quincy City Hall, turn left onto Temple Street. Follow for 100 yards and then turn right onto Washington Street.

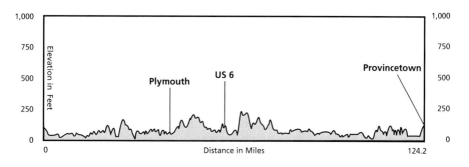

The author and his PMC riding team in 2006 with three-time Tour de France champion Greg LeMond

PAN MASS CHALLENGE
An institution in Massachusetts, the Pan Mass Challenge (PMC) is an epic cycling adventure, spanning nearly 200 miles of challenging terrain over the course of a two-day ride. The challenge for this annual event is not the ride, however. The organization's goal is to raise money to find a cure for cancer, and it has made great progress toward that goal. In its twenty-six-year history, the PMC has raised more than 145 million dollars to fund cancer research at the Dana Farber Cancer Institute in Boston. The nation's most successful athletic fundraiser, the PMC is also a model of efficiency, contributing well over 90 percent of all monies raised to the Dana Farber's Jimmy Fund. More than 4,000 cyclists participate each year, choosing one of three routes, which cross the state on the first weekend in August. The majority of riders follow the "classic" route from Sturbridge to Provincetown. To find out more about the PMC, visit the Web site www.pmc.org or call (800) WE-CYCLE to join the ride or sponsor a rider.

9.5 Keep straight onto SR 3A (Washington Street).

13.7 Keep left onto SR 3A (Broad Cove Road).

14.3 Bear right onto SR 3A (Otis Street).

14.9 Bear left onto SR 3A (Summer Street).

15.0 At roundabout, take the second exit onto SR 3A (Chief Justice Cushing Highway).

25.1 Keep straight onto SR 3A (Main Street).

30.2 Turn left onto State Route 139 (SR 3A).

30.7 Turn right onto SR 3A (Moraine Street).

32.6 Keep straight onto SR 3A (Enterprise Street).

33.3 Keep straight onto SR 3A (Tremont Street).

38.0 Turn left onto SR 3A (Summer Street).

40.0 Keep straight onto SR 3A (Main Street).

41.3 Keep straight onto SR 3A (Court Street).

43.6 Keep straight onto SR 3A (Main Street).

43.7 Bear left onto SR 3A (Main Street Extension).

43.8 Keep straight onto SR 3A (Sandwich Street).

44.0 Turn right onto South Street.

45.3 Road name changes to Long Pond Road (South Street).

45.4 Keep straight onto Long Pond Road.

54.2 Bear left onto Hedges Pond Road.

56.0 Bear right onto SR 3A (State Road).

57.1 Bear left onto Old Plymouth Road.

58.9 Turn right onto Meetinghouse Lane.

59.3 Bear left onto SR 3A (Meetinghouse Lane).

59.4 At roundabout, take the third exit onto US 6 (Mid-Cape Highway).

60.2 At exit 1, keep right onto ramp.

60.4 Road name changes to US 6 (Mid-Cape Connector).

60.8 Turn right onto SR 6A (Old King's Highway).

61.8 Keep straight onto SR 6A (Sandwich Road).

62.2 Keep straight onto SR 6A.

64.4 Keep right onto Charles Street.

65.4 Bear left onto State Route 130 (Water Street).

65.7 Turn left onto Service Road.

72.3 Turn left onto State Route 149 (Prospect Street), then immediately turn right onto Service Road.

74.2 Turn left onto Oak Street.

75.2 Keep straight onto State Route 132 (Iyannough Road).

75.3 Bear right onto SR 6A (Main Street).

83.2 Bear right onto Setucket Road.

86.8 Road name changes to Satucket Road.

88.7 Bear right onto Stony Brook Road.

89.5 Keep straight onto SR 6A (Cranberry Highway).

96.1 Turn left onto Main Street.

96.3 Road name changes to Rock Harbor Road.

98.1 Turn left onto Bridge Road.

99.7 Keep left onto Herring Brook Road.

99.9 Keep left to stay on Herring Brook Road.

102.8 Turn left onto Massasoit Road.

104.3 Road name changes to West Road.

104.9 Turn left onto US 6 (State Highway).

107.5 Turn right onto Old County Road (Old Kings Highway).

107.9 Bear right onto Old County Road.

108.1 Bear left remaining on Old County Road (Old Kings Highway).

109.4 Turn left onto Cahoon Hollow Road.

109.9 Turn right onto US 6 (State Highway).

117.5 Bear left onto SR 6A (Shore Road).

122.1 Keep straight onto SR 6A (Commercial Street).

123.0 Keep left onto Commercial Street.

123.1 Keep left to stay on Commercial Street.

124.2 Arrive at the Provincetown Chamber of Commerce.

Ride Information

Local Information

Greater Boston Convention & Visitors Bureau, 2 Copley Place, Suite 105, Boston; (888) SEE-BOSTON, (617) 536-4100; www.boston usa.com.

Plymouth County Convention & Visitors Bureau, 32 Court Street, 2nd Floor, Plymouth; (800) 231-1620, (508) 747-0100; www.see plymouth.com.

Provincetown Chamber of Commerce, 307 Commercial Street, Provincetown; (508) 487-3424.

Local Events and Attractions

Pan Massachusetts Challenge, 77 Fourth Avenue, Needham; (781) 449-5300; www.pmc.org

Restaurants

Anthony's Pier 4 Restaurant, 140 Northern Avenue, Boston; (617) 482-6262.

Black Rose, 160 State Street, Boston; (617) 742-2286.

Pete's Dockside, 660 Summer Street, Boston; (617) 423-1110.

Accommodations

Boston Marriott Long Wharf, 296 State Street, Boston; (617) 227-0800.

Provincetown Inn, 1 Commercial Street, Provincetown; (508) 487-9500.

Seaport Hotel, One Seaport Lane, Boston; (877) SEAPORT, (617) 385-4000.

Map

DeLorme Massachusetts Atlas & Gazetteer, pages 41, 53, 54, 58-59, 60, 61, 65, 66-67.

26 Marion Ramble

The Marion Ramble is a flat and enjoyable one-town ride which explores Marion, Massachusetts. Traversing the peninsula of the Sippican Harbor, named for the Indian tribe that once lived there, you'll enjoy wonderful coastal scenery, including many stunning estates. You'll also visit the uniquely un-commercialized town center of Marion, which was developed in the 1800s primarily as a home port for sea captains and sailors.

Start: Corner of Spring and Main Streets in the center of Marion. Park where legal on Spring Street, facing north, across from either the town hall or the elementary school.

Length: 17.4 miles.
Ride time: 1 hour.
Terrain: Flat.
Traffic and hazards: Quiet coastal roads.

Getting there: From Interstate 195 South, take exit 20 (State Route 105, Marion). Turn right (south) at end of ramp and go about 0.5 mile to fork where Front Street bears left and Spring Street bears right. Bear right for 0.2 mile to U.S. Route 6. Go straight for 0.9 mile to end (Main Street).

This is a one-town ride on which you explore Marion, one of the series of water-front communities along Buzzards Bay between the Rhode Island border and the Cape Cod Canal. Midway between New Bedford and the canal along both sides of Sippican Harbor, Marion is a yachting center and the site of Tabor Academy, a pres-tigious private school. The expansive harbor divides the town into two portions, with the center of town on the western shore. On the eastern shore of the harbor is Sippican Neck, a peninsula rimmed with estates and large, gracious homes. One of the estates, Great Hill, matches anything to be found along the Massachusetts coast. It makes up its own 300-acre subpeninsula, with a majestic mansion over-looking the bay, narrow lanes hugging the shore, and a hill 125 feet high with spec-

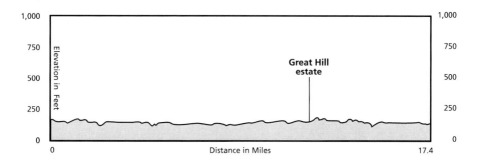

Sippican Harbor, Marion

tacular views. Unfortunately, the estate is open only on weekdays from 9:00 A.M. to 3:00 P.M. It's worth doing this ride during the week just to see the estate.

The ride starts off by going through the unspoiled, untouristed center of town, with a white Victorian town hall, several churches, and cedar-shingled homes and shops. You'll bike along the shoreline, passing Tabor Academy with its Tudor-style main building directly on the water. From here you'll swing over to Sippican Neck, bike to its tip along traffic-free roads, and return along its opposite shore, passing the Great Hill estate.

Miles and Directions

0.0 Head east down Main Street, away from Spring Street and toward the shore.

0.3 Turn right (southeast) onto Water Street.

0.8 Turn right on Lewis Street.

1.0 Bear right (northwest) onto Front Street.

2.5 Turn right (northeast) onto US 6 (Wareham Road).

3.2 Turn right (east) onto Creek Road.

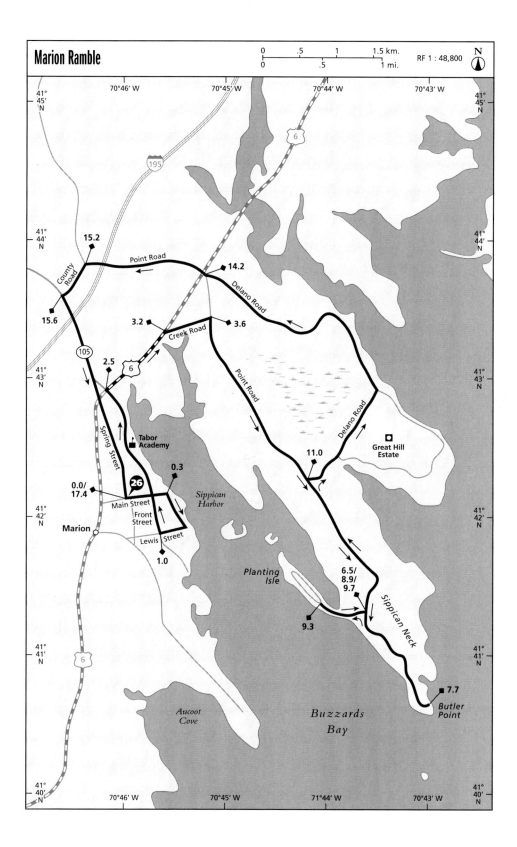

3.6	Turn right (south) onto Point Road. Continue to Butler Point.
7.7	Turn around at Butler Point.
8.9	Turn left (west) onto Planting Island Road.
9.3	Turn around.
9.7	Turn left (north) onto Point Road.
11.0	Turn right (northeast) onto Delano Road.
14.2	Turn right (north) onto Point Road.
15.2	Turn left (southwest) onto County Road.
15.6	Turn left (south) onto SR 105 (Front Street).
16.3	Keep right onto Spring Street.
17.4	Arrive back at start.

Ride Information

Local Information

Bristol County Convention & Visitors Bureau, 70 North Second Street, New Bedford; (508) 997-1250.

Plymouth County Convention & Visitors Bureau, 32 Court Street, 2nd Floor, Plymouth; (800) 231-1620, (508) 747-0100; www.see plymouth.com.

Restaurants

Frigate Steak House, 806 Mill Street, Marion; (508) 748-0970.

Sippican Cafe, 167 Spring Street, Marion; (508) 748-0176.

Accommodations

Hillside Motel, 92 Marion Road, Mattapoisett; (508) 758-3396.

Harborview Inn, 13 South Boulevard, Onset; (508) 295-4123.

Map

DeLorme Massachusetts Atlas & Gazetteer, page 64.

27 Dartmouth Ramble

Dartmouth is the fourth-largest town in Massachusetts and home to the University of Massachusetts at Dartmouth. The Dartmouth Ramble explores its numerous back roads, which are ideal for cycling. The landscape of the route is flat, with broad stretches of farmland and salt marshes. The ramble explores the generous coastline of Apponagansett Bay and unique area attractions, such as the Lloyd Environmental Center.

Start: Ponderosa Steakhouse, U.S. Route 6 and Tucker Road in North Dartmouth.
Length: 27.2 miles.
Ride time: 2 hours.

Terrain: Flat, with a couple of gradual, easy hills.
Traffic and hazards: Quiet coastal roads.

Getting there: From Interstate 195 take exit 12 (the Faunce Corner-North Dartmouth exit), and turn south at the end of the ramp. Go 1 mile to US 6. Turn left onto US 6; Ponderosa is just ahead on the right.

The ride starts in North Dartmouth, the commercial center of the town and home of the University of Massachusetts at Dartmouth. The bold, modern campus is about 1 mile off the route. You'll head down to the picturesque village of Padanaram on Apponagansett Bay, with antiques shops and fine old homes. From here you'll cross the bridge over the bay and enjoy bicycling along its shore. You also pass near the marvelous Children's Museum, one of the best in New England.

From Padanaram you'll work your way to the southern coast and the tiny village of Russells Mills on winding, wooded roads. The focal point of Russells Mills is Davoll's General Store, a wonderful country store built in 1793. You'll pass the Lloyd Center for Environmental Studies, dramatically located on Buzzards Bay at the mouth of the Slocum River. Nature trails wind through the grounds, and there's a spectacular view from the top of the main building.

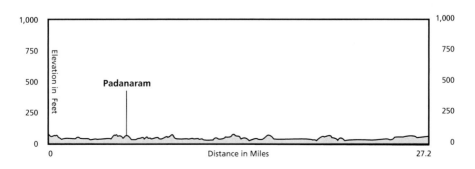

Riders along the Dartmouth coastline

The ride then heads farther into Dartmouth to the Westport town line, passing broad, well-tended farms. Demarest Lloyd Memorial State Park is about 1 mile from the route and worth visiting. It's a lovely expanse of woods and shoreline, with a good beach that doesn't get as crowded as nearby Horseneck Beach.

Miles and Directions

0.0 Depart Ponderosa Steakhouse.

0.1 Turn right onto Tucker Road.

3.1 Turn left onto Russells Mills Road.

4.3 Turn right onto Elm Street.

5.6 Turn right onto Bridge Street.

5.7 Road name changes to Gulf Road.

6.0 Turn left onto Smith Neck Road.

9.3 Turn right onto Little River Road.

10.2 Road name changes to Potomska Road.

12.7 Keep straight onto Rock O'Dundee Road.

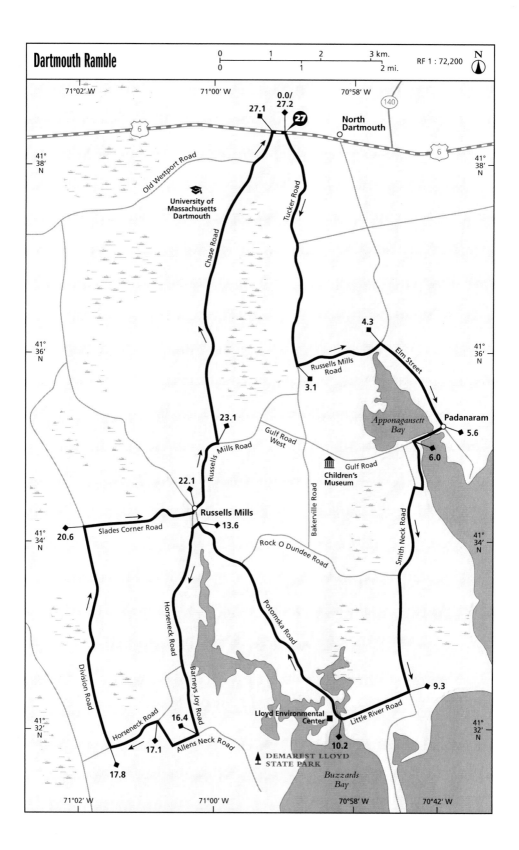

Dartmouth Ramble

RF 1 : 72,200

N

0   1   2   3 km.
0   1   2 mi.

13.6	Turn left onto Tannery Lane, then immediately turn left onto Horseneck Road.
15.6	Keep straight onto Barney's Joy Road.
16.4	Turn right onto Allens Neck Road.
17.1	Turn left onto Horseneck Road.
17.8	Turn right onto Division Road.
20.6	Turn right onto Slades Corner Road.
22.1	Turn left onto Russells Mills Road.
23.1	Turn left onto Chase Road.
26.7	Keep straight onto Old Westport Road.
27.1	Turn right onto US 6 (State Road).
27.2	Arrive back at Ponderosa Steakhouse.

Ride Information

Local Information

Bristol County Convention and Visitors Bureau, 70 North Second Street, P.O. Box 976, New Bedford; (508) 997-1250.

Restaurants

Outback Steakhouse, 349 State Road, North Dartmouth; (508) 994-3700.

Panera Bread, 84 North Dartmouth Mall, North Dartmouth; (508) 994-3700.

Accommodations

Comfort Inn, 171 Faunce Corner Road, North Dartmouth; (508) 996-0800; www.comfort inndartmouth.com.

Holiday Inn Express Hotel and Suites—Harborfront, 110 Middle Street, Fairhaven; (508) 997-1281.

Map

DeLorme Massachusetts Atlas & Gazetteer, page 63.

28 Westport River Ramble

A gently rolling tour of the Westport River along both banks, the Westport River Ramble is an easy, enjoyable ride. Follow the river out to the ocean and back, enjoying scenery that includes vineyards, causeways, and stunning views of Buzzards Bay. The ride never leaves Westport's boundaries and explores all that the town has to offer.

Start: Tennis courts behind Westport Middle School.
Length: 20.4 miles.
Ride time: 1.5 hours.

Terrain: Gently rolling, with one tough hill.
Traffic and hazards: Traffic can be heavy in peak beach season.

Getting there: From State Route 24, head east on Interstate 195 for 2 miles to State Route 88 South. Go 3.5 miles and turn left onto Old County Road at second traffic light. Travel 0.6 mile to school on left.

The Westport River Ramble is a gently rolling landscape of little-traveled country roads winding past snug, cedar-shingled homes with trim picket fences, flawless lawns, and broad meadows sloping gently down to wide tidal rivers and salt marshes. This ride takes you exploring the heart of this area, heading along the east bank of the East Branch of the Westport River, a broad tidal estuary, and returning along the west bank. You'll stay within the borders of Westport, a slender town stretching from I–195 to the ocean at Horseneck Beach, among the most unspoiled in the state. With its splendid harbor and the broad reaches of both the east and west branches of the river, Westport is an active boating center.

The ride starts from the broad, gradual hillside stretching along the river and descends to its narrow northern end. You'll go by the Westport Vineyard and Winery, open most afternoons for tours and tastings. The ride down to Horseneck is delightful, and when you reach the ocean, the road hugs the shoreline for nearly a mile. Just before the main portion of the beach, you'll ride along a causeway to Gooseberry Neck, a small sliver of land that extends into Buzzards Bay. At the far end of the beach, you'll enjoy superb views of the harbor from the bridge across the mouth of the river. Near the end you'll go along the top of the ridge that runs along the west bank of the river, enjoying splendid views of the river below and the neighboring ridge on the other side.

Miles and Directions

0.0 Leave Westport Middle School and head east along Old County Road (away from SR 88).
0.4 Turn right onto Pine Hill Road.
2.5 Turn right to stay on Pine Hill Road.

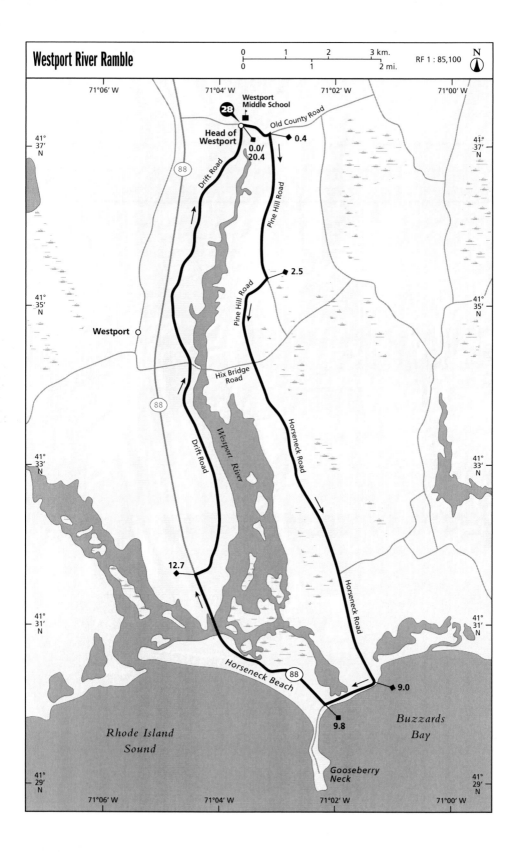

Westport River Ramble

RF 1 : 85,100

N

A placid ocean view at the end of the Westport River

2.6 Keep straight to stay on Pine Hill Road.

3.9 Road name changes to Horseneck Road.

9.0 Turn right at the end onto East Beach Road.

9.8 Turn right onto John Reed Road.

11.5 Bear right (north) onto SR 88.

12.7 Turn right (east) onto Drift Road.

19.8 Turn right (east) onto Old County Road.

20.4 Arrive back at Westport Middle School.

Ride Information

Local Information

Bristol County Convention & Visitors Bureau, 70 North Second Street, New Bedford; (508) 997-1250.

Restaurants

R & S Variety, 488 Old County Road, Westport; (508) 636-5035.

Accommodations

Hampton Inn, 53 Old Bedford Road, Westport; (508) 675-8500.

Map

DeLorme Massachusetts Atlas & Gazetteer, page 63.

29 Lakeville Ramble

Ten miles north of New Bedford is a cluster of large, unspoiled lakes surrounded by woods, prosperous farms, and a few cranberry bogs. Lightly traveled roads threading among the lakes make this one of the nicest regions for biking in southeastern Massachusetts.

Start: Savas Plaza, Lakeville.
Length: 27.2 miles.
Ride time: 2 hours.

Terrain: Gently rolling, with two short hills.
Traffic and hazards: Rural, low-traffic roads that are great for cycling.

Getting there: From Interstate 495, exit south on State Route 18 and go 4 miles to shopping center on right. It's just south of the traffic light where State Route 105 North turns left.

The ride starts from the rural town of Lakeville, which is accurately named. Most of Assawompset Pond and adjacent Long Pond, two of the larger lakes in the state, lie within its borders. Lakeville is unusual in that it has no distinct town center; the closest approximation is where the ride starts. The combination town hall and fire station, housed in a handsome brick building with a bell tower, is close to the starting point. A little beyond is a fine church overlooking the water.

You start off by going along the shore of Assawompset Pond, which, along with most of the other lakes in the area, supplies Taunton and New Bedford with water. Shortly you'll weave between Great Quittacas and Little Quittacas Ponds, both surrounded by pine groves. On the south shore of Little Quittacas Pond is the graceful stone New Bedford Waterworks building; just ahead the lane carves through a perfectly groomed, symmetrical row of trees.

For a few miles you'll ride past small farms and a couple of cranberry bogs on narrow lanes. Then you'll cross the New Bedford Reservoir to the little village of Long Plain (part of the town of Acushnet), which is surrounded by broad farms. It contains a museum of local history housed in a fine Victorian building dated 1875. A little farther along, you'll pass Snipatuit Pond and bike across the gracefully curving causeway between Great Quittacas Pond and Assawompset Pond. At the end you'll go along the latter pond back to the start.

Miles and Directions

0.0 Depart Savas Plaza and head south down SR 105 (SR18).
2.7 Keep straight onto SR 105 (Bedford Street).
4.9 Turn right onto Negus Way.
6.0 Turn left onto SR 18 (Middleboro Road).
6.5 Turn left onto Morton Road.

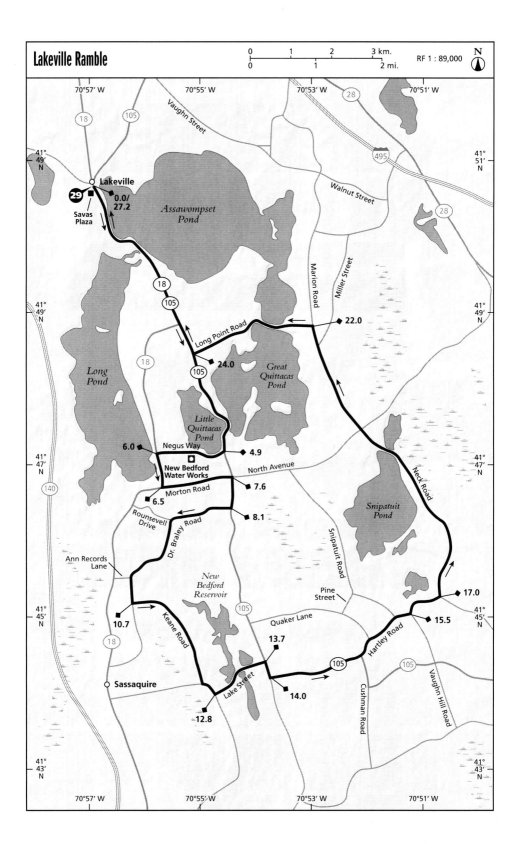

Lakeville Ramble

0   1   2   3 km.
0   1   2 mi.

RF 1 : 89,000

N

70°57′ W   70°55′ W   70°53′ W   70°51′ W

18   105   Vaughn Street   28

495

41° 49′ N

Walnut Street

41° 51′ N

28

Lakeville

29   0.0/ 27.2

Savas Plaza

Assawompset Pond

Marion Road

Miller Street

18
105

41° 49′ N

Long Point Road   ◄   ◆ 22.0

41° 49′ N

18
105   ◆ 24.0

Great Quittacas Pond

Long Pond

Little Quittacas Pond

Neck Road

6.0 ◆   Negus Way   ◆ 4.9

41° 47′ N

New Bedford Water Works   North Avenue

41° 47′ N

140

◆ 7.6

■ 6.5   Morton Road

Snipatuit Pond

◆ 8.1

Rounsevell Drive

Dr. Braley Road

Ann Records Lane

Snipatuit Road

New Bedford Reservoir

105

Pine Street

■ 17.0

41° 45′ N

■ 10.7

Keane Road

Quaker Lane

■ 15.5

41° 45′ N

18

13.7 ■

Hartley Road

Sassaquire

Lake Street

14.0 ■

105   105

Cushman Road

Vaughn Hill Road

■ 12.8

41° 43′ N

41° 43′ N

70°57′ W   70°55′ W   70°53′ W   70°51′ W

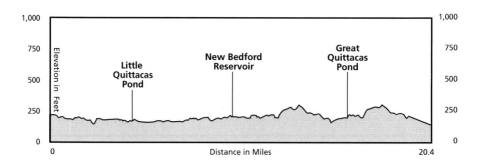

7.1   Road name changes to North Avenue.

7.6   Turn right onto SR 105 (Braley Hill Road).

8.1   Turn right onto Dr. Braley Road.

10.2   Road name changes to Keene Road.

10.7   Turn left to stay on Keene Road.

10.9   Keep straight to stay on Keene Road.

12.5   Turn left onto Peckham Road.

12.6   Road name changes to Middle Road.

12.8   Turn left onto Lake Street.

13.7   Turn right onto SR 105 (Main Street).

14.0   Turn left onto SR 105 (Robinson Road).

15.5   Keep straight onto Hartley Road.

17.0   Bear left onto Gifford Road (Neck Road).

18.1   Road name changes to Neck Road.

20.7   Road name changes to Marion Road.

22.0   Turn left onto Long Point Road.

24.0   Turn right onto SR 105 (Bedford Street).

24.5   Keep straight onto SR 105 (SR 18).

27.2   Arrive back at Savas Plaza.

Ride Information

Local Information

Plymouth County Convention & Visitors Bureau, 32 Court Street, 2nd Floor, Plymouth; (800) 231-1620, (508) 747-0100; www.see plymouth.com.

Restaurants

Country Whip Ice Cream, 1173 Main Street, Acushnet; (508) 763-8051.

Accommodations

Fairfield Inn, 4 Chalet Road, Middleboro; (508) 946-4000.

Courtyard-Boston Raynham, 37 Paramount Drive, Raynham, (508) 822-8383.

Map

DeLorme Massachusetts Atlas & Gazetteer, pages 57, 58.

30 Norton Ramble

Midway between Taunton and Attleboro, about 30 miles south of Boston, is a very enjoyable area for biking. The terrain is nearly level, with an extensive network of little-traveled country roads looping past ponds and prosperous farmland. The region is far enough from Boston to be fairly rural, without much infiltration of suburban development.

Start: Wheaton College visitors parking lot, Norton.
Length: 28.6 miles.
Ride time: 1.5 to 2 hours.
Terrain: Flat to gently rolling.

Traffic and hazards: Most of the ride is along quiet roads. The first section along State Route 140 can be busy. Care must be taken when crossing Interstate 495, and on the short segment on State Route 118.

Getting there: Norton is about 2 miles west of I-495. Take exit 10 (State Route 123) and head west for about 1.8 miles to parking lot on right.

The Norton Ramble starts from Norton, one of the most pleasantly rural towns within commuting distance of Boston and a graceful New England classic. The centerpiece of the community is Wheaton College, a high-quality school with a lovely campus graced by elegant, ivy-covered wood and brick buildings. A small pond with a footbridge across it adds to the beauty of the setting. Adjacent to the campus are a stately white church and a handsome brick turn-of-the-century former library.

Near the beginning of the ride, you'll ride along the Norton Reservoir and pass the Tweeter Center, the scene of many popular concerts. Just ahead you'll follow the north shore of the reservoir and go through the small lakeside community of Norton Grove. After a few miles of woods and farmland, you pass Winnecunnet Pond, Watson Pond, and Lake Sabbatia in quick succession. Across from the latter pond is the Paul A. Dever School, an institution for children who have mental disabilities and a port of embarkation for troops during World War II. Watson Pond and Lake Sabbatia are just over the town line in Taunton, a city of 40,000 covering a wide area in the southeastern part of the state. The city, best known for the manufacture of fine silver products, is rural around its outer edges. You'll bike through a pleasant, tree-shaded residential area and then quickly get back into the undeveloped western edge of the city. The return run to Norton brings you through a fine mixture of woods, farmland, and old wooden houses.

Miles and Directions

0.0 Take a right out of the Wheaton College visitors parking lot onto SR 123 (East Main Street), heading toward SR 140.

0.3 Turn right onto SR 140 (Mansfield Avenue).

Norton Ramble

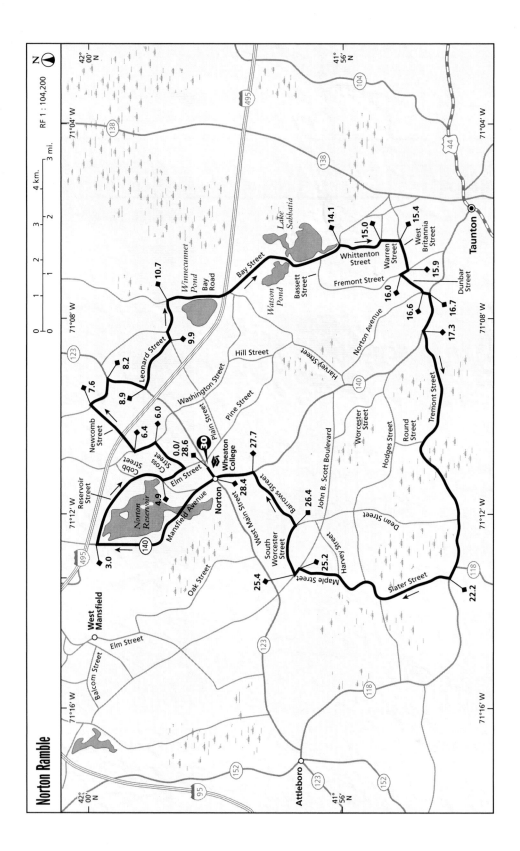

The author and other members of the WGA Cycling Team

2.7	Keep straight onto SR 140 (South Main Street).
3.0	Turn right onto Reservoir Street.
4.9	Turn left onto Elm Street.
5.3	Turn left onto Cross Street.
6.0	Turn left onto North Washington Street.
6.4	Turn right onto Newcomb Street.
7.6	Turn right onto Newland Street.
8.2	Turn right onto SR 123 (East Main Street).
8.9	Turn left onto Leonard Street.
9.9	Turn left onto Plain Street.
10.7	Turn right onto Bay Road.
11.5	Road name changes to Bay Street.
14.1	Turn right onto Whittenton Street.
15.0	Turn right onto Warren Street.
15.4	Turn right onto West Britannia Street.
15.9	Turn right onto Fremont Street.
16.0	Turn left onto Dunbar Street.
16.6	Bear left onto Norton Avenue.
16.7	Turn right onto SR 140 (Tremont Street).

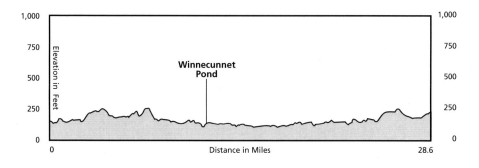

17.3 Bear left onto Tremont Street.

21.9 Keep straight onto SR 118 (Tremont Street).

22.2 Turn right onto Slater Street.

24.3 Road name changes to Maple Street.

25.2 Bear right onto Maple Street Extension, then immediately turn left onto John B. Scott Boulevard.

25.4 Turn right onto South Worcester Street.

26.4 Turn left onto Barrows Street.

27.7 Bear left onto SR 140 (Taunton Avenue).

28.4 Turn right onto SR 123 (East Main Street).

28.6 Arrive back at Wheaton College visitors parking lot.

Ride Information

Local Information

Bristol County Convention & Visitors Bureau, 70 North Second Street, New Bedford; (508) 997-1250.

Restaurants

Alberto's Italian Kitchen, 241 Mansfield Avenue, Norton; (508) 339-2202.
A Nossa Casa Restaurant, 4 Bay Road, Norton; (508) 285-7481.
Jeffrey's Pizza, 63 East Main Street, Norton; (508) 285-5518.

Accommodations

Holiday Inn Taunton-Foxboro, 700 Myles Standish Boulevard, Taunton; (508) 823-0430.

Restrooms

1.8 McDonald's.

Map

DeLorme Massachusetts Atlas & Gazetteer, pages 56-57.

31 Sharon Cruise

A great tour of the flatlands of southeastern Massachusetts, the Sharon Cruise wanders through quiet back roads of Sharon, Mansfield, Norton, and Foxboro. From the quaint suburbia of downtown Sharon, the route visits area attractions such as the Great Woods/Tweeter Center outdoor concert facility, which has hosted many major national and international acts during its twenty years of operation, and the more recently built Norton Country Club, home of the Tournament Player's Club of Boston's annual PGA Tour golf tournament. Most roads along the route are flat and pass through quiet residential or wooded areas with little traffic.

Start: Downtown Sharon, in front of Starbucks coffee shop.
Length: 39.5 miles.
Ride time: 2 to 2.5 hours.

Terrain: Mostly flat with a few small hills toward the end of the ride.
Traffic and hazards: Primarily quiet residential or wooded roads with only short stretches on a couple of busier roads.

Getting there: From Interstate 95 South, take the Coney Street exit (State Route 27) toward Sharon and follow for approximately 2.5 miles to Sharon center. There is free public parking around back of Starbucks. Parking is limited to three hours, but that should allow plenty of time for the ride and a cup of coffee.

Based on a route designed by the Sharon Road Bike Club, the Sharon Cruise is a great tour of suburban towns south of Boston. The roads are mostly quiet, passing through residential neighborhoods and wooded areas, though there is ample opportunity to visit some major area attractions.

Sharon is a quiet bedroom community located equidistant from Boston, Massachusetts, and Providence, Rhode Island. Each state capital is just 22 miles away. This picturesque town has a classic New England hilltop town center complete with white churches and small retail shops, making it a great place to start and end the ride.

After you sweep down past Massapoag Lake and Borderland State Park, you'll find yourself on the back roads of Mansfield, passing the municipal airport before emerging along the more developed area along State Route 140. Here you'll pass the Great Woods/Tweeter Center outdoor concert area. Built more than twenty years ago, this 19,900-seat amphitheatre has hosted a plethora of world-renowned acts, with the type of groups ranging from James Taylor to Avril Lavigne.

In Norton you'll pass by the town's scenic reservoir and its world-class golf course. Opened in June 2002, this Tournament Players Club (TPC) of Boston's PGA Tour course was designed by Arnold Palmer and has been the annual host of the Deutsche Bank U.S. Championship since 2003.

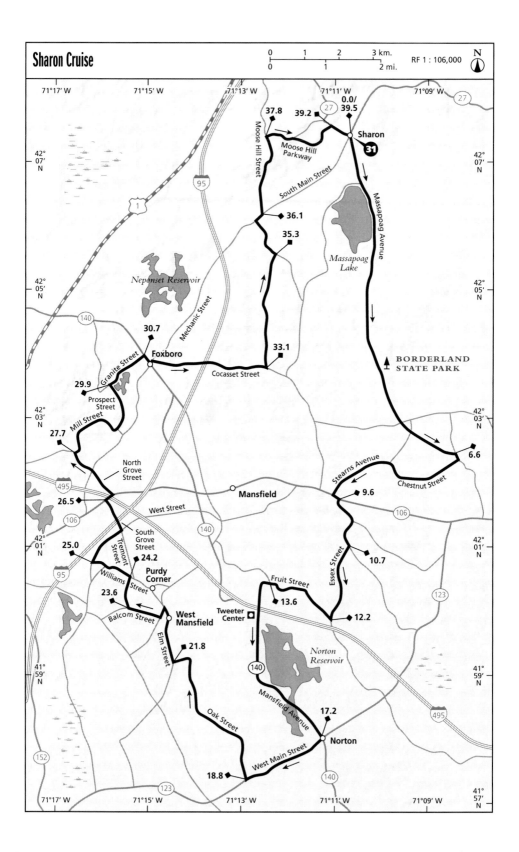

Sharon Cruise

0   1   2   3 km.
0   1   2 mi.

RF 1 : 106,000

N

The route follows great country roads into the center of Foxboro, where professional cyclist and lifelong Massachusetts resident Mark McCormack currently resides. McCormack is quite an accomplished racer, having won the USPRO Road Championship in 2003 and twice reigning as U.S. National Cyclocross Champion, so if you see him along the way on the Sharon Cruise, you likely won't see him for long.

On your way back to Sharon, you'll ride up Moose Hill Street, a great winding road with a bit of a challenging incline. Your reward is a fun descent down Moose Hill Parkway before making the final climb back into Sharon center.

Miles and Directions

0.0 Depart Starbucks, 5 Post Office Square, Sharon.

0.1 Turn right (south) onto Pond Street.

0.9 Turn right (south) onto Massapoag Avenue.

6.6 Bear right (south) onto Poquanticut Avenue.

6.7 Turn right (west) onto Chestnut Street.

8.3 Road name changes to Stearns Avenue.

9.5 Turn left (southeast) onto State Route 106 (East Street).

9.6 Turn right (south) onto East Street.

10.1 Keep right onto Mill Street.

10.7 Turn right (southwest) onto Essex Street.

12.2 Turn right (north) onto North Washington Street.

12.4 Road name changes to Fruit Street.

13.6 Keep straight onto Hall Street.

13.9 Bear left (south) onto South Main Street.

14.1 Road name changes to SR 140 (South Main Street).

14.9 Road name changes to Mansfield Avenue.

17.2 Turn right (southwest) onto State Road 123 (West Main Street).

18.8 Turn right (north) onto Oak Street.

21.8 Turn right (north) onto Elm Street.

22.8 Turn left (south) onto Otis Street.

23.0 Turn right (west) onto Balcom Street.

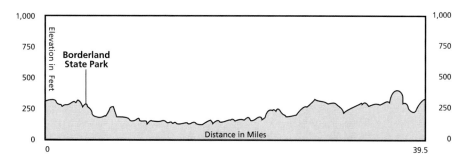

23.6 Turn right (north) onto Jewell Street.

24.2 Turn left (west) onto Williams Street.

24.7 Keep straight onto Pine Street.

25.0 Turn right (north) onto West Street.

25.9 Turn left (northwest) onto South Grove Street.

26.5 Turn right (northeast) onto SR 106 (Green Street).

26.7 Turn left (northwest) onto North Grove Street.

27.3 Road name changes to West Street.

27.7 Turn right (east) onto Mill Street.

29.0 Keep straight onto Prospect Street.

29.9 Turn right (northeast) onto Granite Street.

30.7 Turn right (southeast) onto Market Street.

30.9 Turn left (north) onto South Street.

31.0 Turn right (east) onto Cocasset Street.

33.1 Turn left (north) onto Cannon Forge Drive.

34.0 Road name changes to Forge Road.

34.3 Turn right (northeast) onto Grape Shot Road.

34.6 Keep straight onto Gavins Pond Road.

34.7 Turn right onto Furnace Street.

35.3 Turn left (northwest) onto Wolomolopoag Street.

35.9 Turn right (northeast) onto South Main Street.

36.1 Turn left (north) onto Moose Hill Street.

37.8 Turn right (east) onto Moose Hill Parkway.

39.2 Turn right (southeast) onto SR 27 (Upland Road).

39.5 Arrive back at Starbucks.

Ride Information

Local Information

Greater Boston Convention & Visitors Bureau, 2 Copley Place, Suite 105, Boston; (888) SEE-BOSTON, (617) 536-4100; www.boston usa.com.

Restaurants

Bickford's Family Restaurant, 973 Providence Highway, Sharon; (781) 784-8633.

Pizzigando, 1 Pond Street, Sharon; (781) 784-8161.

Accommodations

Holiday Inn Express Sharon, 395 Old Post Road, Sharon; (781) 784-1242.

Saphire Manor & Inn, 56 Highland Avenue, Sharon; (781) 784-2400.

Restrooms

15.7 McDonald's.

Map

DeLorme Massachusetts Atlas & Gazetteer, page 52.

32 Foxboro Ramble

Home to many accomplished Massachusetts cyclists, Foxboro and the surrounding towns offer many enjoyable, cycling-friendly roads. Don't be surprised to see other cyclists along the route, particularly if you head out on a weekend morning, as there are many active clubs in the area. You may even catch a glimpse of professional racer Mark McCormack or other well-known local cyclists Tobi Shultze and Mike Fairhurst along the wooded, winding roads of the Foxboro Ramble.

Start: Foxboro town green.
Length: 23.1 miles.
Ride time: 1.5 hours.
Terrain: Gently rolling, with a few short hills.

Traffic and hazards: Use caution passing by the Interstate 95 on and off ramps on Robert F. Toner Boulevard and along the brief section of U.S. Route 1, a very busy road.

Getting there: If you're heading south on I-95, take the South Main Street–Mechanic Street exit (exit 8). Turn right at end of ramp, go about 2.5 miles to the Foxboro green, and park on the far side of the green. If you're heading north on I-95, exit north onto State Route 140, go about 1.5 miles to the Foxboro green, and park on the opposite side of the green. There are no time restrictions on parking on SR 140 South facing the green on the left side of the road.

On this ride you will explore the rural, lake-dotted countryside just south of the midpoint between Boston and Providence. You start from Foxboro, an attractive town with two fine churches and a green forming a central square. A landmark in the town is a small, ornate building that was constructed as a Civil War memorial and for many years served as the town library. From Foxboro you'll head through tidy residential areas to Plainville, a pleasant rural town consisting mainly of woods, farmland, and orchards. You'll bicycle along two unspoiled ponds, Turnpike Lake and Lake Mirimichi, and return to Foxboro along forested narrow lanes.

You'll then head south into Mansfield, a compact mill town surrounded by countryside. The route stays in the rural western part of Mansfield, avoiding the center of town. You'll pass Greenwood Lake and then the North Attleboro National Fish Hatchery, a fascinating spot to visit if open (its hours are limited). You'll descend steeply into Plainville then emerge near Turnpike Lake.

Miles and Directions

0.0   From the Foxboro town green, head south down South Street.
2.3   Turn left onto North Grove Street.
2.9   Turn right onto State Route 106 (Green Street).
3.1   Turn left onto South Grove Street.

The beginning of fall foliage season at Greenwood Lake PHOTO BY MICHAEL FAIRHURST

3.7 Road name changes to Tremont Street.

4.6 Bear left onto Williams Street.

5.0 Turn right onto Old Elm Street.

5.3 Turn right onto School Street.

5.5 Bear right onto Otis Street.

6.6 Turn right onto Gilbert Street.

7.7 Turn left onto West Street.

8.0 Road name changes to Mansfield Road.

8.5 Turn right onto Bungay Road.

9.0 Bear left onto State Route 152 (Kelley Boulevard).

10.3 Keep straight onto SR 152 (North Main Street).

10.4 Turn right onto Robert F. Toner Boulevard.

10.8 Turn right onto John L. Dietsch Boulevard.

11.4 Turn left onto Towne Street.

12.2 Turn right onto Commonwealth Avenue.

12.5 Turn right onto Mount Hope Street.

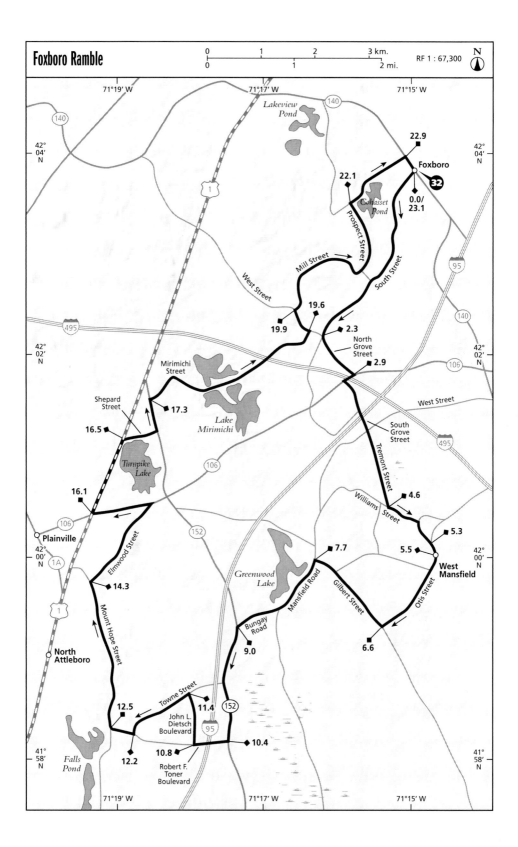

Foxboro Ramble

0   1   2   3 km.

0   1   2 mi.

RF 1 : 67,300

N

71°19' W   71°17' W   71°15' W

140

Lakeview Pond

140

42° 04' N

42° 04' N

22.9

1

Foxboro

32

22.1

Cohasset Pond

0.0/ 23.1

Prospect Street

95

Mill Street

South Street

West Street

19.6

140

19.9

2.3

North Grove Street

42° 02' N

2.9

106

42° 02' N

Mirimichi Street

West Street

17.3

Shepard Street

Lake Mirimichi

South Grove Street

16.5

495

Turnpike Lake

Tremont Street

16.1

106

4.6

106

152

Williams Street

5.3

Plainville

5.5

42° 00' N

1A

Elmwood Street

Greenwood Lake

7.7

West Mansfield

42° 00' N

14.3

1

Mansfield Road

Gilbert Street

Otis Street

North Attleboro

Mount Hope Street

Bungay Road

9.0

6.6

12.5

Towne Street

11.4

152

John L. Dietsch Boulevard

95

12.2

10.8

10.4

41° 58' N

Falls Pond

Robert F. Toner Boulevard

41° 58' N

71°19' W   71°17' W   71°15' W

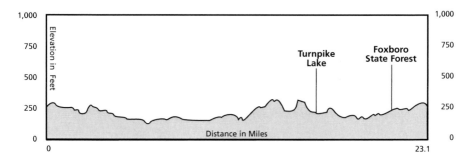

14.3 Turn right onto Elmwood Street.

15.0 Road name changes to Messenger Street.

15.4 Turn left onto SR 106.

15.6 Turn right onto George Street.

16.1 Turn right onto US 1 (Washington Street). Caution: Very busy road.

16.5 Bear right onto Shepard Street.

17.0 Turn left onto Taunton Street.

17.3 Turn right onto Mirimichi Street.

18.6 Road name changes to Mirimichi Road.

19.6 Turn left onto West Street.

19.9 Turn right onto Mill Street.

21.2 Keep straight onto Prospect Street.

22.1 Turn right onto Granite Street.

22.9 Turn right onto SR 140 (Main Street), then immediately turn right onto School Street.

23.1 Arrive back at Foxboro town green.

Ride Information

Local Information

Greater Boston Convention & Visitors Bureau, 2 Copley Place, Suite 105, Boston; (888) SEE-BOSTON, (617) 536-4100; www.bostonusa.com.

Restaurants

Commons Eatery & Cafe, 20 Central Street, Foxboro; (508) 543-4432.

Old Country Store, 26 Otis Street, Mansfield; (508) 339-8128.

Accommodations

Courtyard-Boston Foxborough, 35 Foxboro Boulevard, Foxboro; (508) 543-5222.

Map

DeLorme Massachusetts Atlas & Gazetteer, pages 52, 56.

33 Hopkinton Cruise

The Hopkinton Cruise is a hilly tour of the less-traveled roads of Hopkinton, Hopedale, Mendon, Uxbridge, Upton, and Westborough. This rural area explores the wonderful suburbs between Worcester and Boston just outside the Interstate 495 beltway along the west side of the Blackstone River Valley. The area is rich in great cycling roads and in history, including the starting point for the oldest marathon in the country, if not the world, the Boston Marathon, first run in 1897.

Start: Ash Street, Hopkinton.
Length: 42.5 miles.
Ride time: 3 to 3.5 hours.
Terrain: Hilly.

Traffic and hazards: Most of the route is on quiet back roads, though it occasionally crosses a busy road.

Getting there: I-495 South to exit 21A onto West Main Street. Follow West Main Street for 2.2 miles (becomes State Route 135/Main Street) and turn right onto Ash Street. There's free parking along the common.

Originally run out of neighboring Ashland in 1897, just one year after the first modern Olympic Games, the Boston Marathon was founded and run with a fifteen-member field. In the years since its humble beginnings, the Boston Marathon has become a world-class event that attracts top athletes from around the globe. The current field size has grown to more than 20,000 athletes.

The start of the race was moved to Main Street in Hopkinton in 1927, right near the start of the Hopkinton Cruise. When the marathon route was moved, it was also lengthened to 26 miles, 385 yards to match the new standard for Olympic marathons, set in 1908 when the Olympic Games were held in London. The change was made to accommodate the wishes of King Edward VII and Queen Alexandria. They wanted the race to begin at Windsor Castle so that the royal family could view the start. The distance to Olympic Stadium, including the track finish, proved to be exactly 26 miles, 385 yards, and every Olympic marathon since 1908 has been exactly that distance.

Rather than head for Boston, however, the Hopkinton Cruise is going to take you through the rolling back roads of Hopkinton and surrounding towns in the Blackstone River Valley. The Blackstone River Valley covers some twenty-four communities and an area of 400,000-plus acres and is known as the birthplace of the American Industrial Revolution. The Blackstone River drops 438 feet over 46 miles, and as such, it generated a lot of water power that helped transform the area from farm to industry.

In spite of sparking an economic boom, the area clings to its rural roots and has preserved several natural resources in the process. The Hopkinton Cruise will take you

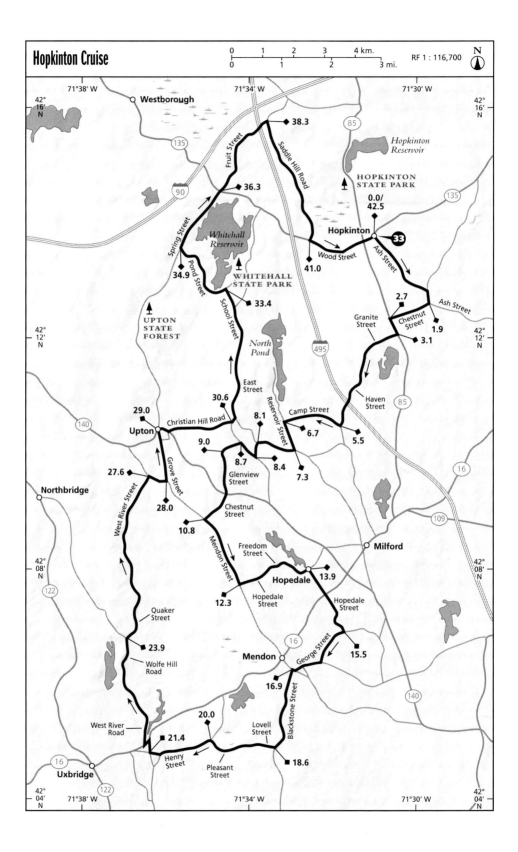

Hopkinton Cruise

0 1 2 3 4 km.
0 1 2 3 mi.
RF 1 : 116,700

N

Westborough

38.3

36.3

34.9

33.4

41.0

30.6

29.0
Upton

27.6

28.0

23.9

21.4

20.0

18.6

16.9

15.5

13.9

12.3

10.8

9.0

8.7

8.4

8.1

7.3

6.7

5.5

2.7

1.9

3.1

0.0/
42.5

Hopkinton

33

Northbridge

Uxbridge

Mendon

Milford

Hopedale

HOPKINTON
STATE PARK

WHITEHALL
STATE PARK

UPTON
STATE
FOREST

Whitehall
Reservoir

Hopkinton
Reservoir

North
Pond

Fruit Street
Saddle Hill Road
Spring Street
Pond Street
School Street
East Street
Reservoir Street
Wood Street
Ash Street
Ash Street
Granite Street
Chestnut Street
Haven Street
Camp Street
Christian Hill Road
Grove Street
West River Street
Glenview Street
Chestnut Street
Mendon Street
Freedom Street
Hopedale Street
Hopedale Street
George Street
Blackstone Street
Quaker Street
Wolfe Hill Road
West River Road
Henry Street
Pleasant Street
Lovell Street

71°38' W
71°34' W
71°30' W

42° 16' N
42° 12' N
42° 08' N
42° 04' N

135
90
85
135
495
85
16
109
140
122
16
122
16
140

by Hopkinton State Park, a 1,450-acre area reserved for hiking, biking, nonmotorized boating, skiing, picnicking, horseback riding, snowmobiling, and swimming. The route also passes along the east side of Upton State Forest, a 2,600-acre forest with many trails for hiking, biking, and horseback riding. You will cruise along the west side of Whitehall State Park, which is made up almost entirely of water. The 592-acre Whitehall Reservoir, once used for drinking water, now supports boating and fishing, along with offering hiking trails.

The route is challenging with frequent climbs, but it also offers some great quiet roads and a chance to see the countryside along infrequently traveled roads of these suburbs.

Miles and Directions

0.0 Depart Ash Street on the east side of the town common by the Center School. Head southeast down Ash Street.

1.8 Turn right at stop sign, remaining on Ash Street.

1.9 Turn right at stop sign onto Chestnut Street.

2.7 Turn left onto State Route 85 (Hayden Rowe Street).

3.1 Turn right onto Granite Street (marked, but sign is hard to see).

3.8 Bear left onto Lumber Street. Caution: Lumber Street is very narrow and rough for the first 100 yards, with a short dirt section.

4.3 Road name changes to Haven Street.

4.8 Turn left to stay on Haven Street.

5.5 Turn right onto Purchase Street.

5.7 Turn left onto Camp Street.

6.7 Turn left onto Reservoir Street.

7.3 Turn right onto Whitewood Road.

8.0 Road name changes to East Street.

8.1 Turn left onto Pond Street (marked, but sign is on the right-hand side of the road and not very visible).

8.4 Turn right onto Fiske Mill Road (not marked).

8.7 Turn left onto Tyler Road.

9.0 Bear left onto Glenview Street.

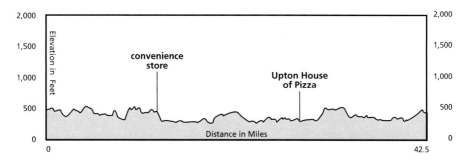

10.1 Go straight across State Route 140 (Milford Street) onto Chestnut Street.

10.8 Turn left onto Mendon Raod (not marked).

11.8 Road name changes to North Avenue.

12.3 Turn left onto Hopedale Street.

12.9 Road name changes to Freedom Street.

13.9 Turn right onto Hopedale Street.

14.1 Cumberland Farms.

15.1 Turn right onto Green Street.

15.5 Turn right onto Mill Street.

15.9 Road name changes to George Street.

16.3 Turn right to stay on George Street.

16.4 Keep straight to stay on George Street.

16.8 Road name changes to Main Street.

16.9 Turn left onto Blackstone Street.

18.6 Bear right onto Lovell Street (marked but sign on opposite side of the street).

19.1 Road name changes to Pleasant Street as you cross Millville Street.

20.0 Bear left onto Park Street.

20.6 Road name changes to Henry Street.

21.4 Turn right onto Patrick Henry Street (marked on opposite side of street).

21.5 Road name changes to West River Road.

23.0 Turn right onto Upton Street.

23.6 Road name changes to Wolfe Hill Road.

23.9 Turn right onto Quaker Street.

24.8 Road name changes to Moonhill Road.

24.6 Road name changes to West River Street.

27.6 Bear right onto Mendon Street (not marked).

28.0 Bear left onto Grove Street.

29.0 Turn right onto SR 140 (Milford Street).

29.1 Upton House of Pizza.

29.2 Turn left onto Elm Street (not marked).

29.3 Bear right onto Christian Hill Road.

30.6 Turn left onto Fiske Mill Road, then immediately bear left onto East Street.

31.8 Road name changes to School Street.

33.4 Turn left onto Pond Street.

34.9 Bear right onto Spring Street.

36.3 Bear right onto SR 135 (Wood Street), then immediately bear left onto Cunningham Street.

36.6 Turn left onto Fruit Street (not marked).

38.3 Turn right onto Saddle Hill Road.

40.8 Road name changes to Walker Street.

41.0 Turn left onto SR 135 (Wood Street).

41.8 Bear left onto SR 135 (Main Street).

42.5 Turn right onto Ash Street and arrive back at town common.

Ride Information

Local Information
Central Massachusetts Tourist Council, 30 Worcester Center Boulevard, Worcester; www.worcester.org.

Restaurants
Bill's Pizza & Restaurant, 14 Main Street, Hopkinton; (508) 435-0447.
Dynasty Chinese Restaurant, 77 West Main Street, Hopkinton; (508) 435-8088.
Upton House of Pizza, 6 Milford Street, Upton; (508) 529-6666.

Accommodations
Courtyard-Boston Milford, 10 Fortune Boulevard, Milford; (508) 634-9500.
Guestmark International Inc, 11 Grove Street, Hopkinton, (508) 435-7169.

Map
DeLorme Massachusetts Atlas & Gazetteer, pages 39, 51.

34 Whitinsville Challenge

The Whitinsville Challenge weaves through a hilly and scenic section of the Blackstone Valley just above the Rhode Island state border. Tour the quiet back roads of Douglas, Uxbridge, Mendon, and Millville along the Blackstone River. Get a stunning view of the Whitin Reservoir and enjoy many challenging back roads in this hilly section of Massachusetts that is home to some of the state's most important history related to the Industrial Revolution.

Start: Whitin Community Center, Whitinsville.
Length: 46.3 miles.
Ride time: 3 to 3.5 hours.
Terrain: Very hilly.

Traffic and hazards: Mostly quiet back roads. Some stretches are along busier numbered routes, which for the most part have wide shoulders.

Getting there: Take Interstate 495 South to exit 21B and take a right at the end of the ramp onto West Main Street. Follow for about 4 miles and take a left onto School Street. Take a right at the end of School Street onto Pleasant Street (not the sharp right onto Main Street) and follow for 4 miles (Pleasant Street becomes Quaker Street). Take a right onto Church Street and travel for 1.5 miles. Take a right onto Hill Street and an immediate left into the Whitin Community Center parking lot.

The Whitinsville Challenge travels through Northbridge, a growing suburban town made up of several villages, including Linwood, Northbridge, Riverdale, Rockdale,

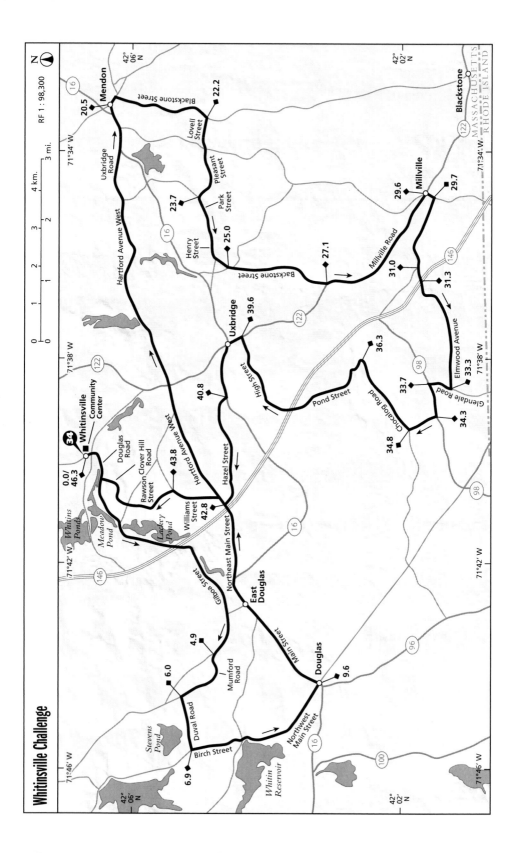

Whitinsville Challenge

RF 1 : 98,300

Placid country road along the Whitinsville Challenge route

and Whitinsville, in the Blackstone River Valley of south-central Massachusetts.

Over the course of several generations, the Whitin family built their fortune manufacturing textile machinery and milling cotton. Eventually an entire community was formed around the very successful Whitinsville Cotton Mill and the Whitin Machine Works enterprises. The community thrives to this day as one of the villages of Northbridge, Massachusetts. Located in the heart of the Blackstone River Valley, an epicenter of the Industrial Revolution in Massachusetts, Northbridge and the surrounding area offer wonderful winding and rolling roads perfect for cycling.

The Whitinsville Challenge first offers a tour of Douglas, a quiet town of 7,500 residents, to take in a stunning view of the Whitin Reservoir, which stretches more than 1.5 miles from east to west. You'll loop back through the center of East Douglas, where you can pick up extra snacks or drinks, before heading due east to Mendon center. Use caution on this stretch of the ride along Hartford Avenue, as it can be busy with traffic. The shoulders are fairly wide most of the way, but the speed limit increases to more than 40 mph for cars along this road.

You'll leave Mendon center along Blackstone Street, which is one of the nicest roads along the route. These very rural back roads will eventually lead you down along the Blackstone River. You'll take a brief ride down State Route 122 on the final run into Millville. SR 122 can be busy also, but the shoulder is very wide and visibility is good along this downhill section. In Millville, you'll cross over the Blackstone River and begin weaving your way back up some really great country roads on the way to the center of Uxbridge. From here it's a short ride back to the Whitinsville start.

Miles and Directions

0.0 Depart Whitinsville Community Center by taking a right out of the parking lot onto Hill Street.

0.1 Proceed straight through traffic light. Road name changes to Douglas Road.

2.9 Road name changes to Gilboa Street.

4.1 Keep straight onto Manchaug Road.

4.9 Keep left onto Mumford Road.

6.0 Turn left onto Duval Road.

6.9 Turn left onto Torrey Road.

7.1 Road name changes to Birch Street.

7.8 Road name changes to Northwest Main Street.

9.2 Bear left onto Church Street.

9.6 Turn left onto Common Street, then immediately bear left onto State Route 16 (Main Street).

11.9 Bear left onto Northeast Main Street.

12.4 Road name changes to Hartford Avenue West.

19.6 Turn left onto SR 16 (Uxbridge Road).

20.2 Bear right onto Maple Street.

20.5 Bear right onto Main Street.

20.6 Turn right onto Blackstone Street.

22.2 Bear right onto Lovell Street.

22.8 Road name changes to Pleasant Street.

23.7 Bear left onto Park Street.

24.3 Road name changes to Henry Street.

25.0 Turn left onto Blackstone Street.

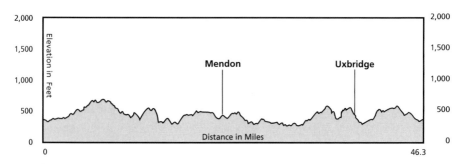

27.1 Bear left onto SR 122 (Millville Road).

29.6 Turn right onto Central Street.

29.7 Turn right onto Ironstone Street.

30.3 Road name changes to River Road.

31.0 Keep left onto Balm of Life Spring Road.

31.3 Turn left onto Ironstone Street, then immediately bear right onto Elmwood Avenue.

33.3 Turn right onto Glendale Road.

33.7 Turn left onto State Route 98 (Aldrich Street).

34.3 Turn right onto Johnson Road.

34.8 Bear right onto Chockalog Street.

36.3 Turn left onto Mill Street.

36.5 Turn left onto Pond Street.

38.2 Keep straight onto High Street.

39.6 Turn left onto SR 122 (South Main Street).

39.8 Turn left onto SR 16 (Douglas Street).

40.8 Turn right onto Cross Road.

40.9 Bear left onto Hazel Street.

42.8 Bear right onto Hartford Avenue West.

43.0 Bear left onto Williams Street.

43.8 Turn left onto Rawson Street.

44.7 Turn left onto McGuire Road, then immediately turn right onto Clover Hill Road.

45.1 Turn left onto Hastings Drive.

45.5 Turn right onto Douglas Road.

46.3 Proceed straight through traffic light. Road name changes to Hill Street.

46.3 Arrive back at Whitinsville Community Center.

Ride Information

Local Information

Central Massachusetts Tourist Council, 30 Worcester Center Boulevard, Worcester; www.worcester.org.

Restaurants

Harry's Famous Pizza, 185 Church Avenue, Northbridge; (508) 234-5155.

Jube's Family Restaurant & Pizza, 1227 Providence Road, Whitinsville; (508) 234-7768.

Mendon Diner, 24 Uxbridge Road, Mendon; (508) 478-9332.

Northbridge House of Pizza, 2225 Providence Road, Northbridge; (508) 234-3936.

Accommodations

Fairfield Inn, 1 Fortune Boulevard, Milford; (508) 478-0900.

Quaker Inn & Conference Center, 442 Quaker Highway, Uxbridge; (508) 278-2445.

Map

DeLorme Massachusetts Atlas & Gazetteer, pages 50-51.

35 Tristate Cruise

The Tristate Cruise is a tour of the very rural, mostly wooded, lake-studded countryside surrounding the point where Massachusetts, Rhode Island, and Connecticut meet. The terrain is not as hilly as in the surrounding areas. The lightly traveled back roads, winding through the woods and along several ponds, promise enjoyable and peaceful bicycling.

Start: Friendly's Ice Cream, Webster.
Length: 34.3 miles.
Ride time: 2.5 hours.

Terrain: Rolling, with one tough hill.
Traffic and hazards: Mostly quiet roads. Care must be taken when crossing Interstate 395.

Getting there: Start at shopping center behind Friendly's Ice Cream on State Route 12 in Webster. From I-395, head west onto State Route 16 (take exit 2). Just ahead go straight at traffic light, and you'll immediately see Friendly's on your right.

The ride starts in Webster, a small Massachusetts mill city on the French River just north of the Connecticut line. You'll immediately head into rolling, wooded countryside to the tiny village of West Sutton and pass Sutton Falls, a small dam with a little covered bridge above it. Just ahead are pleasant roads along Manchaug Pond and then Whitin Reservoir, where you'll pass a waterslide (here's your chance to descend a different type of hill). From here it's a short way to the graceful, classic New England village of Douglas, with a stately white church, old cemetery, and triangular green.

From Douglas you'll follow a smooth secondary road to the attractive little mill town of Pascoag, in the northwestern corner of Rhode Island. Pascoag is typical of the many mill villages hugging the fast-flowing rivers throughout that state. Leaving the town, you'll skirt the Wilson Reservoir and then climb gradually to the top of Buck Hill, one of Rhode Island's highest points.

You now speed down two steep hills into the northeastern corner of Connecticut. After about 3 miles of narrow lanes, you'll cross back into Webster and return into town along the shore of Lake Chargoggagoggmanchaugagoggchaubunagungamaug (usually called Webster Lake), which in the Nipmuc Indian language means, "I fish on my side, you fish on your side, and nobody fishes in the middle." If it hasn't been stolen, a sign spelling out the name of the lake may greet you as you cross the state line.

A shorter ride heads directly from Douglas back to Webster without leaving Massachusetts by following SR 16 West. There's a great descent near the end, and you'll ride along Webster Lake at the bottom.

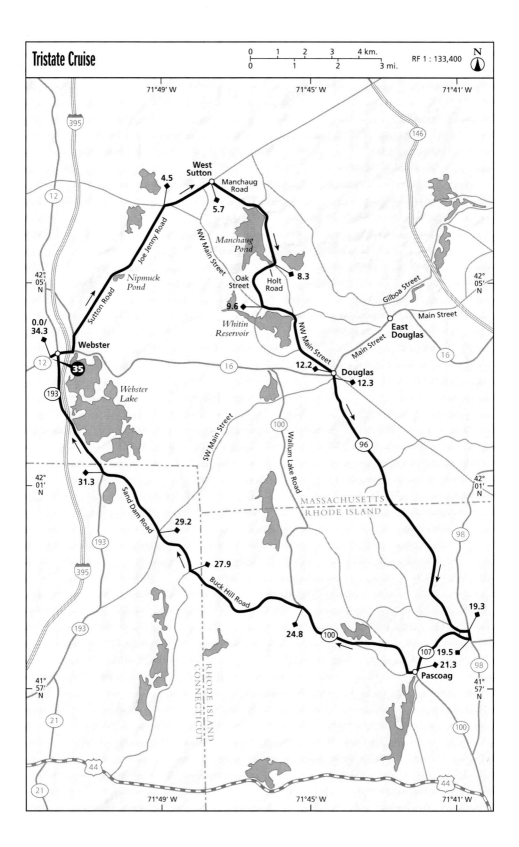

Tristate Cruise

0   1   2   3   4 km.
0   1   2   3 mi.

RF 1 : 133,400

N

71°49' W   71°45' W   71°41' W

395

12

146

West Sutton

4.5

Manchaug Road

5.7

42° 05' N

Nipmuck Pond

Joe Jenny Road

NW Main Street

Manchaug Pond

Oak Street

Holt Road

8.3

42° 05' N

Gilboa Street

Main Street

Sutton Road

0.0/ 34.3

Webster

9.6

Whitin Reservoir

NW Main Street

East Douglas

16

12

35

193

Webster Lake

16

12.2

Douglas

12.3

100

SW Main Street

Wallum Lake Road

96

42° 01' N

31.3

42° 01' N

98

MASSACHUSETTS
RHODE ISLAND

193

29.2

395

27.9

Buck Hill Road

Sand Dam Road

193

19.3

24.8

100

107

19.5

21.3

41° 57' N

RHODE ISLAND
CONNECTICUT

21

44

Pascoag

98

41° 57' N

100

21

44

Miles and Directions

0.0 Depart Friendly's, East Main Street, Webster.

0.1 Keep straight onto SR 16 (East Main Street).

0.4 Turn left onto Sutton Road.

3.1 Road name changes to Cliff Street.

3.2 Road name changes to Joe Jenny Road.

4.5 Turn right onto Sutton Avenue.

5.0 Road name changes to Central Turnpike.

5.7 Bear right onto Manchaug Road.

7.9 Keep straight onto Torrey Road.

8.3 Turn right onto Holt Road.

8.5 Road name changes to Oak Street.

9.6 Bear left onto Northwest Main Street.

11.8 Bear left onto Church Street.

12.1 Bear right onto Common Street.

12.2 Bear right onto State Route 96 (Southwest Main Street).

12.3 Bear left onto SR 96 (South Street).

15.5 Enter Rhode Island.

16.6 Keep straight onto SR 96 (Round Top Road).

18.9 Turn left onto SR 96 (Callahan School Street).

19.3 Turn right onto State Route 98 (Harrisville Main Street).

19.5 Turn right onto Rhode Island Route 107 (Chapel Street).

20.4 Keep straight onto RI 107 (Pascoag Main Street).

21.1 Road name changes to Rhode Island Route 100 (RI 107).

21.3 Turn right onto Bridge Way, follow for 150 yards, then turn left onto Sayles Avenue and immediately right onto RI 100 (High Street).

21.5 Bear right onto RI 100 (Church Street).

22.4 Keep straight onto RI 100 (Wallum Lake Road).

24.8 Bear left onto Wallum Lake Road.

24.9 Bear left onto Buck Hill Road.

27.5 Enter Connecticut.

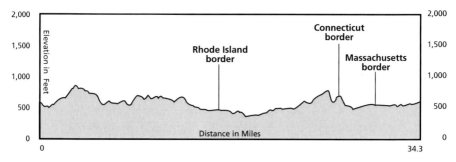

27.9 Turn right onto Quaddick Town Farm Road.

29.2 Bear right onto East Thompson Road, then immediately bear left onto Sand Dam Road.

31.3 Bear right onto Connecticut Route 193 (Thompson Road).

31.5 Enter Massachusetts.

34.2 Turn left onto SR 12 (East Main Street).

34.3 Arrive back at Friendly's.

Ride Information

Local Information
Central Massachusetts Tourist Council,
30 Worcester Center Boulevard, Worcester;
www.worcester.org.

Restaurants
Sutton Falls Camp Inc., 90 Manchaug Road,
Sutton; (508) 865-5883.

Accommodations
Annex East-West Lodge, Webster; (508)
943-8858.
Redwood Motel, 360 Worcester Road, Charlton; (508) 248-5371.

Map
DeLorme Massachusetts Atlas & Gazetteer,
pages 50-51.

36 Brookfields Cruise

On the Brookfields Cruise you explore the four similarly named towns midway between Worcester and Springfield. The surrounding landscape, a harmonious mixture of magnificent rolling farmland, wooded hills, ridges with inspiring views, and several lakes, promises biking at its best along a wide-ranging network of rural lanes and lightly traveled secondary roads. The terrain is not as hilly as the more rugged ridge country surrounding it.

Start: Start at State Route 9 beside Lake Lashaway in the center of East Brookfield.
Length: 27.8 miles.
Ride time: 1.5 to 2 hours.

Terrain: Delightfully rolling, with several short hills and one tough one.
Traffic and hazards: None.

Getting there: The start is about 15 miles west of Worcester. Park along SR 9.

The ride starts in East Brookfield, the smallest and least distinctive of the quartet of towns on the route, attractively located along the shore of Lake Lashaway. A couple of miles out of town is a beautiful ride along Quaboag Pond, the largest lake in the area, followed by another ride beside Quacumquasit Pond (say it three times fast). From here you'll ascend gradually onto a hillside with magnificent views across the

Brookfields Cruise

RF 1 : 97,000

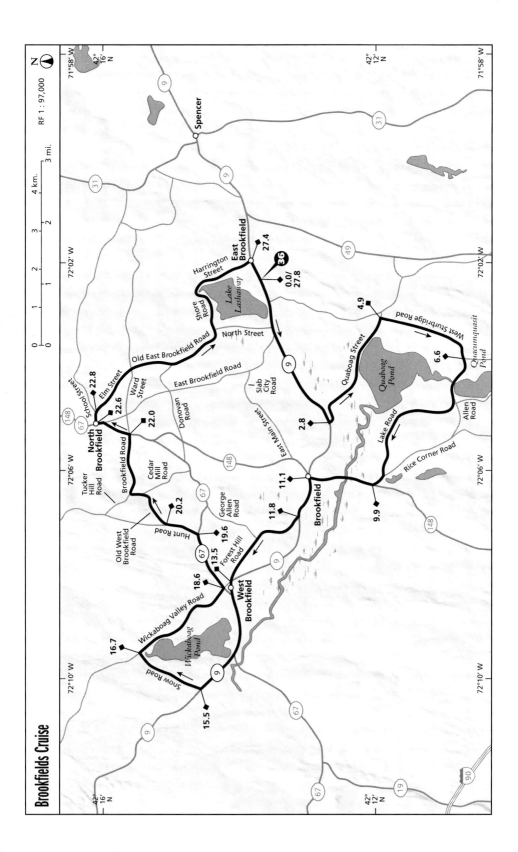

A rider along the Brookfields Cruise route surrounded by the peaceful scenery

well-groomed fields of estates and horse farms. Just ahead you'll cross the Quaboag River and climb a short hill into the classic New England village of Brookfield. The long, slender green is framed by two dignified churches, an ornate brick Victorian library, and fine old homes. Just off the green the compact business block is a relic from the turn of the twentieth century.

Leaving Brookfield, you'll climb onto another ridge with fine views and descend into West Brookfield, the most elegant of the four towns on the ride. The long, triangular green, highlighted by a fountain in the middle, is surrounded by a fine church and gracious wooden and brick homes. Just west of town you'll make a circuit around Wickaboag Pond and thread your way between rolling hills to North Brookfield, yet another New England gem of a town, with a traditional white church; a green, graceful stone library; and an ornate Victorian town hall with a bell tower, built in 1864. A statue on the green honors the soldiers killed in the War of the Rebellion, the official Union name for the Civil War.

From North Brookfield you'll enjoy a relaxing descent through orchards back to the shore of Lake Lashaway and East Brookfield.

Miles and Directions

0.0 Depart East Brookfield, on SR 9 (East Main Street).

2.8 Turn left onto Quaboag Street.

4.3 Road name changes to Shore Road.

4.9 Turn right onto West Sturbridge Road.

6.6 Keep straight onto South Pond Road.

7.0 Road name changes to Lake Road.

7.4 Turn right to stay on Lake Road.

8.1 Keep straight to stay on Lake Road.

9.9 Bear right onto State Route 148 (Fiskdale Road).

10.6 Keep straight onto SR 148 (Upper River Street).

11.1 Turn left onto SR 148 (Common Street), then immediately turn left onto SR 9 (West Main Street).

11.8 Bear right onto West Brookfield Road.

12.1 Road name changes to Forest Hill Road.

13.5 Keep straight onto SR 9 (East Main Street).

13.8 Keep straight onto State Route 67 (SR 9).

14.8 Road name changes to SR 9 (West Main Street).

15.5 Turn right onto Snow Road.

16.7 Turn right onto Wickaboag Valley Road.

18.4 Road name changes to Church Street.

18.6 Turn left onto SR 67 (North Main Street).

19.6 Turn left onto Hunt Road.

20.2 Bear right onto Old West Brookfield Road.

20.4 Near North Brookfield, bear left onto Old West Brookfield Road.

20.9 Turn left to stay on Old West Brookfield Road.

21.1 Turn right onto Bates Street.

22.0 Bear left onto SR 148 (SR 67).

22.6 Turn right onto School Street.

22.8 Keep straight onto Elm Street.

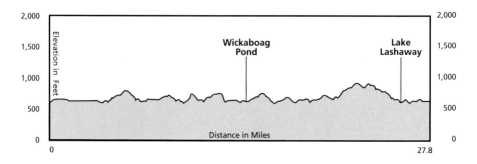

23.7	Road name changes to Old East Brookfield Road.
25.5	Road name changes to Shore Road.
26.3	Turn right to stay on Shore Road.
26.6	Road name changes to Harrington Street.
27.4	Turn right onto SR 9 (East Main Street).
27.8	Arrive back in East Brookfield.

Ride Information

Local Information

Central Massachusetts Tourist Council, 30 Worcester Center Boulevard, Worcester; www.worcester.org.

Restaurants

Trolley Stop Restaurant, 294 East Main Street, East Brookfield; (508) 867-5995.
Uncle Sam's Pizza, East Main Street, East Brookfield; (508) 885-2925.

Accommodations

Copper Lantern Motor Lodge, 184 West Main Street, West Brookfield; (508) 867-6441.
Lashaway Inn, 80 Main Street, East Brookfield; (508) 867-2150.

Map

DeLorme Massachusetts Atlas & Gazetteer, pages 36-37, 48-49.

37 Connecticut River Ramble

The heart of the Pioneer Valley, midway between the Connecticut and Vermont–New Hampshire borders, is the prime tobacco-growing region of Massachusetts. The valley here is broad and flat, with long, weathered tobacco sheds standing guard over the wide, sweeping fields, and with mountains rising in the distance. The Connecticut River Ramble offers a rare flat route in this mountainous region of the state.

Start: Northampton opposite Smith College.
Length: 27.8 miles.
Ride time: 2 hours.
Terrain: Flat.

Traffic and hazards: Quiet country roads. Short segment on State Route 116 can be busy at times.

Getting there: From Interstate 91 North take exit 18 (U.S. Route 5). Go north on US 5 for 1 mile to State Route 9. Turn left for 0.5 mile to Smith College. Park at side of road or on a side street.

Northampton, a city of 30,000, is one of the most attractive communities for its size in New England. In the downtown area (a few blocks off the route), the unusually wide main street is lined with gracious, ornate buildings from the nineteenth century: churches, the county courthouse, city hall, the Forbes Library, old commercial

The flat, tobacco fields of State Route 47

buildings, and many others. It's worth visiting the downtown area on foot after the ride. Adjacent to downtown is Smith College, the largest of the "Seven Sisters" schools, with 2,500 students. The tree-shaded campus mixes gracious buildings in many architectural styles. Behind the campus the Mill River flows over a beautiful little dam with a footbridge just below it.

From Northampton you'll head into tobacco country to Hatfield, among the finest of the Pioneer Valley towns, graced by a stately white church built in 1849, a handsome brick library, and old wooden homes. Many of the homes have plaques stating when they were built, and some go back to the 1700s. From Hatfield you'll continue along the Connecticut River to Sunderland, another gracious New England town. For a real challenge, you can climb South Sugarloaf Mountain and gaze in wonder at a spectacular vista with few equals in the state as the broad sweep of the Pioneer Valley unfolds for miles before you.

From Sunderland you'll parallel the river through extensive tobacco farms to the tiny village of North Hadley, with two old churches and a country store. Just ahead is the Porter-Phelps-Huntington House, an outstanding eighteenth-century residence elaborately furnished by six generations of a prominent family. A little farther on you'll ride alongside the river into Hadley, where you'll pass gracious old houses

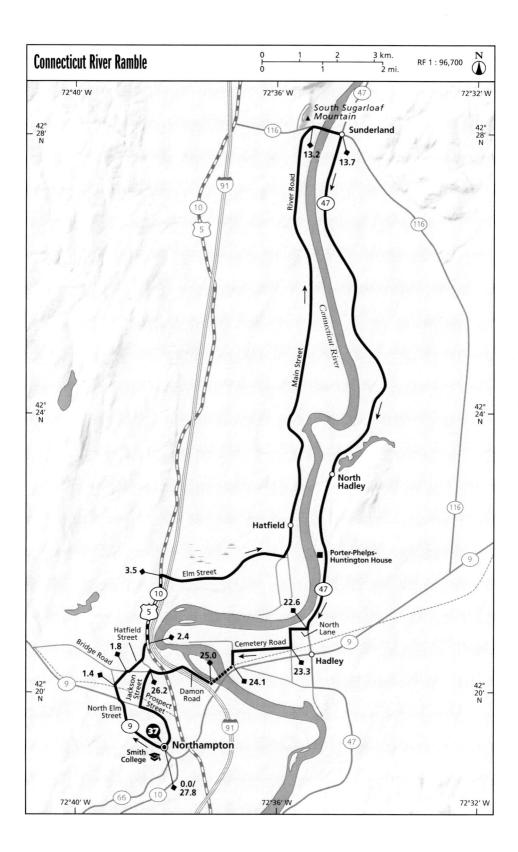

Connecticut River Ramble

RF 1 : 96,700

N

0   1   2   3 km.
0   1   2 mi.

72°40' W   72°36' W   72°32' W

42° 28' N

South Sugarloaf Mountain

Sunderland

13.2

13.7

47

91

10

5

River Road

47

42° 24' N

Connecticut River

Main Street

North Hadley

116

Hatfield

3.5   Elm Street

Porter-Phelps-
Huntington House

10

5

22.6

47

North Lane

9

Hatfield Street

2.4

Cemetery Road

9

1.8

25.0

Hadley

24.1

23.3

Bridge Road

1.4

9

42° 20' N

Jackson Street

26.2

Prospect Street

Damon Road

North Elm Street

9

37

91

47

Northampton

Smith College

0.0/ 27.8

66   10

72°40' W   72°36' W   72°32' W

42° 28' N

42° 24' N

42° 20' N

framing a long, slender green. Just beyond Hadley, you'll cross the river back into Northampton on an old railroad trestle that is part of the Norwottuck Rail Trail.

Miles and Directions

0.0 Depart SR 9 (Elm Street), heading west, away from the town center.

1.2 Turn right onto North Elm Street.

1.4 Bear right onto Hatfield Street.

1.8 Bear right onto Bridge Road, then immediately turn left onto Hatfield Street.

2.4 Bear left onto US 5 (State Route 10).

3.5 Bear right onto Allen Road.

3.6 Road name changes to Elm Street.

5.4 Road name changes to Maple Street.

5.7 Bear left onto Main Street.

9.8 Road name changes to River Road.

13.2 Turn right onto SR 116 (Sunderland Road).

13.7 Turn right onto State Route 47 (South Main Street).

14.1 Bear right onto SR 47 (River Road).

15.6 Keep straight onto SR 47 (Hadley Road).

22.5 Keep straight onto SR 47 (Middle Street).

22.6 Turn right onto North Lane.

23.0 Road name changes to West Street.

23.3 Turn right onto Cemetery Road.

24.1 Turn left onto Cross Path Road. Optional: Continue along Cemetery Road to end and follow Norwottuck Rail Trail to cross the river without going on SR 9. You will pick up the route at Damon Road.

24.4 Turn right onto SR 9 (Russell Street).

25.0 Turn right onto Damon Road.

25.9 Road name changes to Bridge Road.

26.2 Turn left onto Jackson Street.

26.8 Turn left onto Prospect Street.

27.8 Turn left onto SR 9 (Elm Street) and arrive at start.

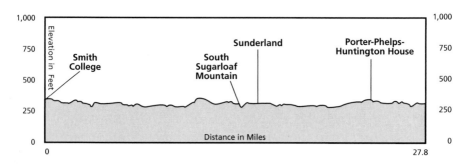

Ride Information

Local Information

Greater Springfield Convention & Visitors Bureau, 1441 Main Street, Springfield; (800) 723-1548, (413) 787-1548.

Restaurants

Millstone Farm Market, 24 South Main Street, Sunderland; (413) 665-0543.
Northampton Brewery, 11 Brewster Court, Northampton; (413) 584-9903.

Accommodations

Clarion Hotel & Conference Center, 1 Atwood Drive, Northampton; (413) 586-1211.
Inn at Northampton, 1 Atwood Drive, Northampton; (413) 586-1211.

Map

DeLorme Massachusetts Atlas & Gazetteer, page 35.

38 Hilltown Challenge

Just northwest of Springfield, delightful bicycling abounds in the small valley tucked between the East Mountain–Mount Tom range on the east and rugged, wooded hill country on the west. Lying in the small watershed of the Manhan River, the valley presents a harmonious blend of broad, gently rolling farms and stands of woodland, with views of the surrounding hills across the fields.

Start: Bickford's Family Restraurant, Westfield.
Length: 36.1 miles (but don't let that fool you, this is a tough one).
Ride time: 2.5 to 3 hours.
Terrain: Very hilly with two big climbs.

Traffic and hazards: Mostly quiet roads, though the numbered routes can get busy at times. Some have narrow shoulders. Care must also be taken when crossing Interstate 90.

Getting there: Take the Massachusetts Turnpike to exit 3, and turn right at end of exit ramp. Bickford's is at State Route 10 and U.S. Route 202.

The ride starts on the outskirts of Westfield, a small industrial city that for many years was best known as the home of Columbia bicycles. You'll immediately head into farm country as you wind along the western edge of the valley on back roads to the handsome town of Southampton, with its magnificent old white church and a brick turn-of-the-twentieth-century library. From here you'll head through prosperous farmland to Pequot Pond and return to Westfield, skirting the base of East Mountain.

The Hilltown Challenge will give you a taste of the rugged hill country that extends across the western quarter of the state. As you struggle across the steep, nearly unpopulated landscape, you'll understand why the hill towns were the last part of the state to be settled. Leaving the valley, you'll climb nearly 1,000 feet to the tiny, unspoiled hilltop town of Montgomery, complete with a little red schoolhouse, a

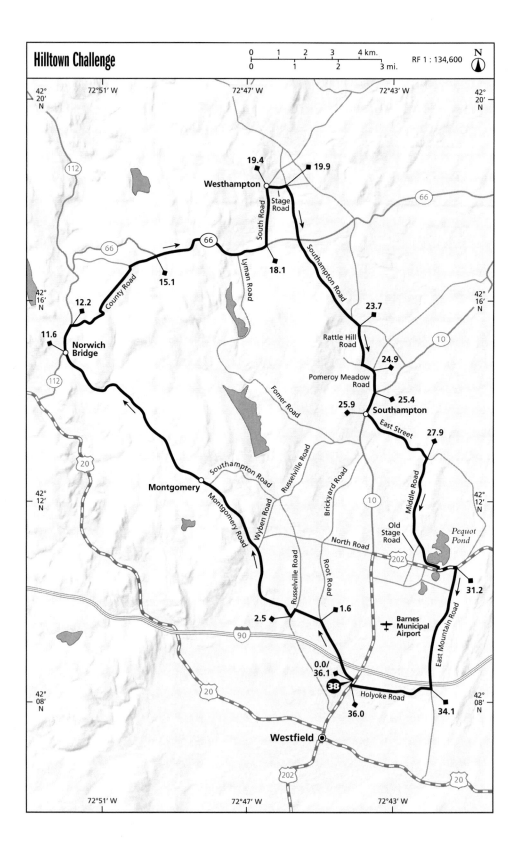

Hilltown Challenge

RF 1 : 134,600

traditional white church, a wooden town hall, and an inviting little library. From here you'll revel in a screaming descent to the Westfield River, only to face another long climb as you head northeast toward Westhampton. This is another New England gem of a town, with a dignified white church commanding the hillside; a small, well-kept green; and a white, pillared town hall. Beyond Westhampton you'll coast primarily downhill to Southampton, enjoying spectacular views of the Mount Tom range. In Southampton you'll pick up the short ride and follow it past Pequot Pond back to Westfield.

Miles and Directions

0.0   Depart Bickford's Family Restaurant onto Arch Road.

0.3   Bear right onto Lockhouse Road.

1.6   Bear left onto Cabot Road.

2.3   Turn left onto Russelville Road.

2.5   Turn right onto Montgomery Road.

5.5   Road name changes to Main Road.

10.7   Road name changes to Montgomery Road.

11.6   Turn right onto State Route 112 (Worthington Road).

12.2   Turn right onto County Road.

13.1   Turn left to stay on County Road.

14.4   Turn right to stay on County Road.

15.1   Turn right onto State Route 66 (Pond Brook Road).

16.2   Keep straight onto SR 66 (Main Road).

18.1   Turn left onto South Road.

19.4   Turn right onto Stage Road.

19.9   Turn right onto Southampton Road.

22.9   Road name changes to Cold Spring Road.

23.4   Turn right to stay on Cold Spring Road.

23.7   Turn right onto Rattle Hill Road.

24.6   Bear left onto Wolcott Road.

24.9   Turn right onto Pomeroy Meadow Road.

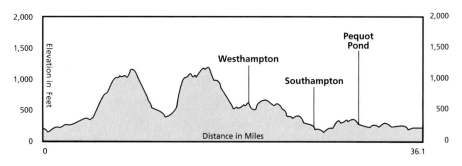

25.4	Turn right onto SR 10 (College Highway).
25.9	Turn left onto East Street.
27.9	Turn right onto Middle Road.
30.0	Road name changes to Long Pond Road.
30.5	Turn left onto Old Apremont Way.
31.0	Turn right, remaining on Old Apremont Way, follow for 50 yards then turn left onto US 202 (North Road).
31.2	Turn right onto East Mountain Road.
34.1	Turn right onto Holyoke Road.
36.0	Keep straight onto US 202 (SR 10).
36.1	Arrive back at Bickford's Family Restaurant.

Ride Information

Local Information

Greater Springfield Convention & Visitors Bureau. 1441 Main Street, Springfield; (800) 723-1548, (413) 787-1548.

Restaurants

Bickford's Family Restaurant, 6 Southampton Road, Westfield; (413) 562-0777.
Outlook Farm Country Store, 136 Main Road, Westhampton; (413) 529-9388.
Paisanos Restaurant & Pizzaria, 136 College Highway, Southampton; (413) 527-8900.

Accommodations

Hotel Westfield, 101 Meadow Street, Westfield; (413) 562-3797.
Westfield Motor Inn, 2 Southampton Road, Westfield; (413) 568-2821.

Map

DeLorme Massachusetts Atlas & Gazetteer, pages 46-47.

39 Great Barrington Challenge

The southwestern corner of Massachusetts abounds with elegant villages and fertile farmland, with views of gently rounded Mount Everett, the second-highest mountain in the Berkshires with an elevation of 2,602 feet, in the distance. The classic New England villages of West Stockbridge and Alford, along with the handsome commercial town of Great Barrington, add variety to the serenely rural area. And, if you like antiques, you're in the right place—the villages of Sheffield and South Egremont boast the highest concentration of antiques shops (most of them in handsome wooden, stone, or brick houses about 200 years old) in the state. Though the Great Barrington Challenge travels along the valley ways between mountains, there's still more than 3,500 feet of climbing to conquer along this scenic half-century route.

Start: The Village School, West Stockbridge.
Length: 52.5 miles.
Ride time: 3 to 4 hours.
Terrain: Rolling with several steep climbs.

Traffic and hazards: U.S. Route 7 in Great Barrington is a busy road, but it has a wide shoulder.

Getting there: From the west, take the Berkshire spur of the New York State Thruway (Interstate 90) to exit B-3 (New York Route 22). Turn left at end of ramp and immediately right onto NY 22 South. Go 0.7 mile to State Route 102 on left. Turn left and travel 2.5 miles to school on right.

From the east, take the Massachusetts Turnpike to exit 1, immediately after the toll booth. Turn right at end of ramp, and just ahead turn left onto SR 102. Follow SR 102 for 0.8 mile to school on left. Park at the ball field on the right-hand side of the school.

The Great Barrington Challenge begins by passing through West Stockbridge, which is not as well-known and much less visited than neighboring Stockbridge, 5 miles to the southeast. The center of the village contains shops and eateries in old wooden buildings and a former train station that now houses retail establishments. You'll follow State Route 41, a gently rolling secondary road with light traffic, for nearly 10 miles to the outskirts of Great Barrington.

Great Barrington, the largest town in southwestern Massachusetts, seems bigger than a community of 7,500. The bustling downtown area boasts several impressive churches and a business district with handsome, three-story brick buildings dating from the late 1800s. The Searles Castle, a forty-room stone mansion built during the 1880s by the widow of railroad tycoon Mark Hopkins, is a downtown landmark. It is now the John Dewey Academy, a school for teenagers with emotional problems. A tough, 0.7-mile-long hill greets you as you leave Great Barrington. About 2 miles out of town is tiny Simon's Rock College, with about 300 students. The college, which enrolls many of its students after their sophomore or junior year of high

Riders at the top of one of the many climbs of the Great Barrington Challenge

school, emphasizes seminar-style education and close relationships between students and faculty. The starkly modern campus is set back about 0.3 mile from the road.

The ride then follows back roads through the nearly level valley of the Housatonic River, passing dairy farms that extend to the river's edge. After about 6 miles you'll come to Sheffield and pass dozens of antiques shops on US 7, the only busy road on the ride (fortunately, it has a wide shoulder). From Sheffield, the route continues along the valley past more dairy farms to the crossroads hamlet of Ashley Falls, where you'll see several more antiques shops in fine old houses. About a mile beyond Ashley Falls is the scenic highlight of the ride, Bartholomew's Cobble, which consists of a pair of small rocky outcroppings that rise about 100 feet above the Housatonic River. Foot trails lead about 100 yards to the first hill and a quarter mile to the second one, affording panoramic views of the meandering river below and mountains in the distance. Just beyond Bartholomew's Cobble is the Colonel Ashley House, the oldest house in Berkshire County, built in 1735. Both the Cobble and the Colonel Ashley House have modest admission fees.

The ride now heads north to South Egremont along SR 41, a beautiful secondary road with the rugged Mount Washington Range (of which Mount Everett is the

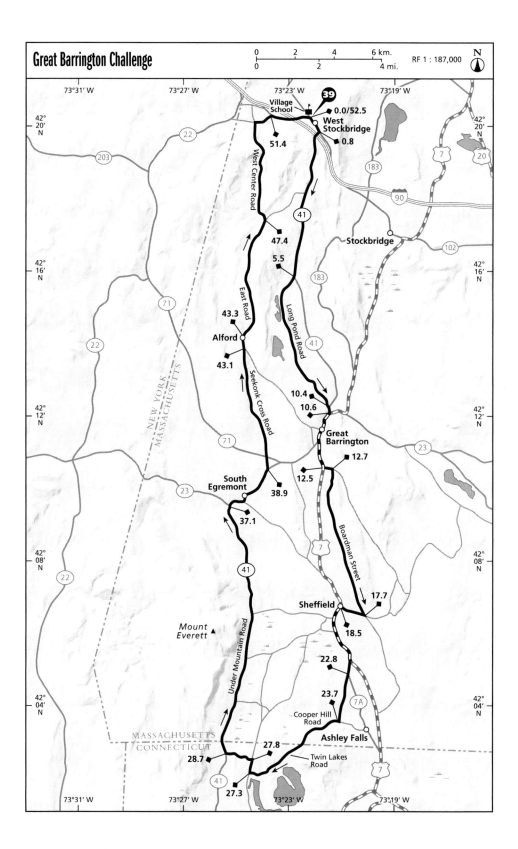

Great Barrington Challenge

RF 1 : 187,000

N

highest peak) on your left, and farms and meadows on your right. You'll pass the handsome brick Stagecoach Hill Inn and then the Berkshire School, a top-quality, coeducational prep school with elegant stone buildings nestled at the foot of Mount Bushnell. South Egremont is a traditional New England village with several antiques shops, the Egremont Inn built in 1780, and a unique little library dating from 1830.

On your way back to West Stockbridge, you'll pass through the picture-book hamlet of Alford, with its graceful church, elegant town hall, and rustic little school-house, all in traditional New England white, located about 3 miles beyond the college. Most of the return trip from Alford back to West Stockbridge follows a beckoning country road that rolls up and down through farmland, with forested hills and mountains in the distance.

Miles and Directions

0.0 Depart Village School on SR 102 (State Line Road).

0.2 Turn right onto SR 102 (SR 41).

0.8 Turn right onto SR 41 (Great Barrington Road).

5.5 Bear right onto Long Pond Road.

8.6 Road name changes to Christian Hill Road.

10.4 Bear right onto SR 41 (North Plain Road).

10.6 Bear right onto US 7 (State Road 23).

12.5 Turn left onto Brookside Road.

12.7 Turn right onto East Sheffield Road.

13.9 Road name changes to Boardman Street.

17.7 Turn right onto Maple Avenue.

18.5 Turn left onto US 7 (Main Street).

20.4 Keep right onto State Route 7A (Ashley Falls Road).

22.8 Turn right onto Rannapo Road.

23.7 Bear left onto Cooper Hill Road.

25.3 Enter Connecticut.

25.3 Road name changes to Twin Lakes Road.

25.9 Keep straight onto Twin Lakes Road.

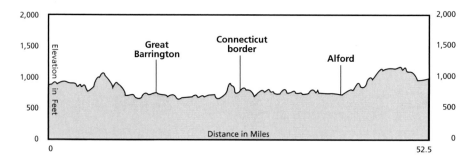

27.3   Turn right onto Taconic Road.

27.8   Turn left onto Hammertown Road.

28.7   Turn right onto SR 41 (Under Mountain Road).

29.1   Enter Massachusetts.

29.3   Keep straight onto SR 41 (South Under Mountain Road).

33.3   Keep straight onto SR 41 (North Under Mountain Road).

35.6   Keep straight onto SR 41 (Under Mountain Road).

37.1   Turn right onto SR 23 (SR 41).

38.9   Turn left onto Seekonk Cross Road.

42.6   Road name changes to Old Great Barrington Road.

43.1   Bear left onto Alford Road.

43.3   Bear right onto East Road.

46.3   Road name changes to East Alford Road.

47.4   Bear left onto West Center Road.

51.4   Turn right onto SR 102 (State Line Road).

52.5   Arrive back at Village School.

Ride Information

Local Information

Discover the Berkshires Visitors Center, 3 Hoosac Street, Adams; (800) 237-5747, (413) 743-4500.

Pittsfield Visitors Center, 121 South Street, Pittsfield; (413) 443-9186; www.berkshires.org.

Restaurants

Caffe Pomo D'Oro, 6 Depot Street, West Stockbridge; (413) 232-4616.

Union Bar & Grill, 293 Main Street, Great Barrington; (413) 528-6228.

The Village Oven, 30 Main Street, West Stockbridge; (413) 232-7269.

Accommodations

Holiday Inn Express Hotel & Suites Great Barrington, 415 Stockbridge Road, Great Barrington; (413) 528-8837.

The Lion's Den, 30 Main Street, Stockbridge; (413) 298-5545.

Map

DeLorme Massachusetts Atlas & Gazetteer, pages 31, 32, 43, 44.

40 New York Border Cruise

Soak up the great scenery of West Stockbridge's historic commercial Main Street, which is made up of a wonderful collection of early nineteenth-century structures, on your way to the placid Queechy Lake, gem of Canaan, New York. A rare treat in the Berkshires, this ride cruises along gently rolling terrain and many long and very enjoyable descents. The price is paid along a single monumental 2.5-mile climb on the way home. Catch your breadth with a relaxing visit to the peaceful Hancock Shaker Village, a living-history museum of twenty buildings on 1,200 acres of farm, fields, meadow, and woodlands.

Start: McDonald's parking lot, Pittsfield.
Length: 33 miles.
Ride time: 2.5 to 3 hours.
Terrain: Rolling hills with many long, beautiful descents, with a single, significant 2.5-mile climb on the latter part of the ride.

Traffic and hazards: The ride travels primarily over quiet roads and/or roads with generous shoulders. Care must be taken on U.S. Route 20, the most heavily traveled of all the roads on this route.

Getting there: Interstate 90 to exit 2, US 20. Follow US 20 west for approximately 13 miles to McDonald's.

Herman Melville wrote *Moby Dick* in his Pittsfield home. And, just as Ishmael yearns for the sea whenever he finds himself "growing grim about the mouth," we cyclists may be equally well-served by the rejuvenating effects of a scenic ride along country roads in the Pittsfield area. The New York Border Cruise provides ample opportunity for relaxing and unwinding on the bike, along with a significant climb near the end of the ride just to make sure you've flushed everything out of your system.

From the convenience of bustling downtown Pittsfield, the New York Border Cruise brings you into downtown West Stockbridge, a town once owned by the Stockbridge Indians until it was sold to European settlers. Unique among towns in the Berkshires, the West Stockbridge's original economy was not totally driven by agriculture. Fine marble and iron ore from its many quarries contributed significantly to the town's early growth. Interestingly, much of the marble used to build the State House in Boston came from the quarries of West Stockbridge. Today you will find a bustling downtown section with many retail shops housed in the towns nineteenth-century buildings.

The New York Border Cruise will take you over the state line to Queechy Lake in Canaan, New York. The winding road along its edge provides spectacular views of the lake and surrounding mountainous countryside. After visiting the

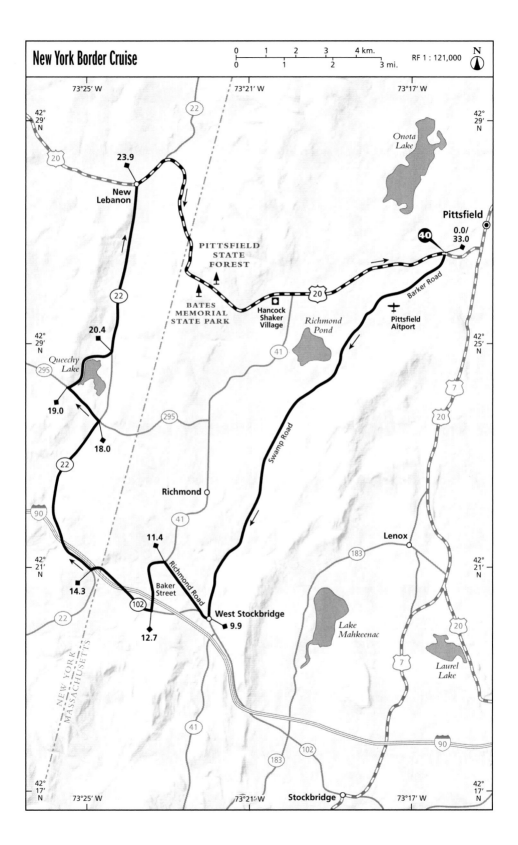

New York Border Cruise

RF 1 : 121,000

N

73°25' W   73°21' W   73°17' W

42° 29' N

22

23.9

New Lebanon

Onota Lake

Pittsfield

40

0.0/ 33.0

20

22

PITTSFIELD STATE FOREST

Barker Road

20.4

42° 29' N

BATES MEMORIAL STATE PARK

Hancock Shaker Village

Richmond Pond

41

Pittsfield Aitport

42° 25' N

Queechy Lake

295

19.0

7

18.0

22

295

20

Swamp Road

90

Richmond

41

Lenox

183

42° 21' N

11.4

Richmond Road

42° 21' N

14.3

Baker Street

Lake Mahkeenac

22

102

West Stockbridge

9.9

12.7

7

20

Laurel Lake

NEW YORK **MASSACHUSETTS**

41

90

102

183

42° 17' N

Stockbridge

42° 17' N

73°25' W   73°21' W   73°17' W

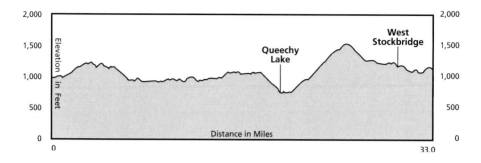

lake, you'll enjoy a long descent along New York Route 22 before heading back toward Pittsfield along US 20. Here is where the big climb of the day occurs. You'll climb steadily along a steep 2.5-mile section of US 20 between Pittsfield State Forest and Bates Memorial State Park. There is a scenic lookout just near the top that provides a great spot to rest. Also, there is a convenient stop for refreshments just down the other side of the hill.

As you finish the ride along US 20, be sure to stop by the Hancock Shaker Village to view its wonderfully preserved 1,200 acres of farm, woodland, and meadow.

Miles and Directions

0.0 Depart McDonald's east onto US 20 (West Housatonic Street).

0.3 Turn right (south) onto Barker Road.

3.4 Road name changes to Pittsfield Road.

4.8 Road name changes to Swamp Road.

9.9 At Swamp Road in West Stockbridge, turn right (west) onto State Route 102 (State Road 41).

10.1 Bear left (northwest) onto SR 41 (Albany Road).

11.4 At Baker Street in Richmond, bear left (west) onto Baker Street.

12.7 Turn right (west) onto SR 102 (State Line Road).

14.1 EnterNew York.

14.1 Road name changes to New York Route 958.

14.3 Turn right (northwest) onto New York Route 22.

18.0 Turn left (northwest) onto New York Route 295.

19.0 Turn right (east) onto New York County Road 30 (Queechy Lake Drive).

20.4 Turn left (north) onto NY 22.

23.9 Turn right (east) onto US 20 (NY 22).

26.6 Enter Massachusetts.

33.0 Arrive back at McDonald's.

Ride Information

Local Information

Discover the Berkshires Visitor Center, 3 Hoosac Street, Adams; (800) 237-5747, (413) 743-4500; www.berkshires.org.
Pittsfield Visitors Center, 121 South Street, Pittsfield; (413) 395-0105.

Accommodations

Bascom Lodge, Summit of Mount Greylock, Adams; (413) 743-1591.
Berkshire Inn Motel, 150 Housatonic Street, Pittsfield; (800) 443-0633 or (413) 443-3000.

Ramada Limited Inn & Suites, 1350 West Housatonic Street, Pittsfield; (877) 477-5817.

Restrooms

0.0 McDonald's.

Map

DeLorme Massachusetts Atlas & Gazetteer, page 32.

About the Author

Motivated by personal loss, Tom Catalini took up cycling as a serious hobby when he began to participate in the annual Pan Mass Challenge bike-a-thon, which raises money for cancer research. The two-day event covers 192 miles from Central Massachusetts to the tip of Cape Cod. Tom has completed the event seven times and raised tens of thousands of dollars to fund cancer research at the Dana Farber Cancer Institute. Tom is also active in the Northeast Bicycle Club, Charles River Wheelmen, North Shore Cyclists, and a variety of other local cycling clubs and group rides. He lives in Melrose with his wife and three children.

For a variety of additional resources on cycling in Massachusetts, visit this book's companion Web site www.RoadBikingMassachusetts.com. In addition to a variety of forums, the Web site offers information about many cycling clubs, group rides, bike racing, and cycling related events happening throughout the state.

The author on the coast along Lynn Shore Drive on the Marblehead Ramble

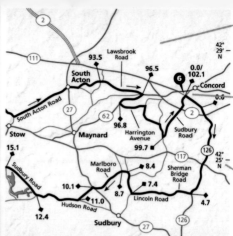

Shaded relief representing terrain indicates slope.

Enhanced detail shows more symbols, labels, and features.

Latitude and longitude number and grid ticks are GPS compatible

Go for a Ride!

"FalconGuides point the compass to the best spots to play, climb, hike, fish, and be." —*CNN*.com

For more than twenty-five years, FalconGuide® has set the standard for outdoor recreation guidebooks. Written by top outdoors experts and enthusiasts, each guide invites you to experience the endless adventure and rugged beauty of the great outdoors.

Road Biking™ Massachusetts features forty carefully designed rides throughout the state, from the summit of Mount Greylock to the tip of Cape Cod and everywhere in between. Local cyclist Tom Catalini provides a sampling of the state's diverse offerings, including rides in the rugged Berkshire Mountains, through scenic Nashoba and Pioneer Valleys, around the historic North Shore, and along Boston's picturesque South Shore to Provincetown.

Look inside to find:

- GPS-compatible, 3-D shaded relief maps
- Rides for evey fitness level and ability, from an easy 17-mile ramble to a challenging 124-mile classic
- Detailed information about each ride, including directions, length, terrain, traffic conditions, and road hazards
- Vivid descriptions of points of interest

Front cover photo © Creatas/Superstock
Back cover photo © Tom Catalini
Cover design by Linda R. Loiewski

FALCONGUIDE®

P.O. Box 480
Guilford, CT 06437
www.falcon.com

Falcon® is an imprint of The Globe Pequot Press

$16.95/Canadian $18.95

ISBN 978-0-7627-3909-7

51695

9 780762 739097